HYDROPONICS GARDENING

This book includes:

The Absolute Beginners Guide +21 Little Known Secrets to Build Your Hydroponic Garden without Soil, Fast and Easy

James Water

First Book:

Hydroponics for Absolute Beginners:

How to Build your Inexpensive Garden without Soil Fast and Easy

Second Book:

Hydroponics:

21 Little-Known Secrets to Build your Hydroponic Garden

Table of Content

Book 1: **Hydroponics for Absolute Beginners**

Book 2: **Hydroponics, 21 Little-Known Secrets**

HYDROPONICS

FOR ABSOLUTE BEGINNERS:

How Build Your Inexpensive Garden

Without Soil Fast and Easy

James Water

Chapter 1

HYDROPONIC CULTIVATION

Hydroponics is a generic term that embraces different cultivation techniques that have as a standard feature the use of water and nutrients to feed plants that are grown "out of the soil" or without using the land.

There are two main methods of hydroponic cultivation; the first foresees the use of "inert" materials or supports whosc purpose is only to support the root system of the plant, the other is the direct immersion of the roots in the nutrient solution.

The advantages of hydroponic without soil cultivation - compared to traditional cultivation techniques - lie above all in the possibility of starting one or more hydroponic crops even in less hospitable environments and in conditions not suitable for the birth and growth of plants. For example, it is indicated in all those places characterized by a high drought or where temperatures are particularly rigid or in areas where the soil under excessively sandy, rocky, or arid.

Amount of water to be provided for irrigation

Another essential aspect of hydroponic cultivation fundamental for fans and professionals of hydroponic gardening is the quantity of water to be provided for irrigation: in traditional crops on the land, the amount of water necessary to be able to cultivate and make the plants fruit is clearly higher compared to that required by vegetables grown in hydroponics. In fact, it is calculated that the ratio is 10 (for traditional crops) to 1 (for hydroponic crops).

Hydroponic culture

The saving of water is reflected both in the economic aspect and on the environmental issue.

In short, hydroponic cultivation - also known as hydroponic culture precisely because it affects different economic, social, and even cultural areas - has a decidedly limited ecological footprint compared to traditional cultivation techniques.

Use of fertilizers, herbicides, and pesticides

Another critical factor is the use of fertilizers, herbicides, and pesticides used and the relative quantities foreseen in the two types of crops: the volumes of fertilizers used are somewhat limited and always well targeted. Furthermore, there is no dispersion of the soil. Herbicides are not used, because they are not necessary, while pesticides are used in small quantities.

Organic Hydroponic cultivation

For those who want to grow organically, it is possible to use organic fertilizers that allow you to have a hydroponic organic culture, respecting health, and the environment.

Why choose a Hydroponic cultivation method?

In a hydroponic system, plants grow out of the ground, in a fully regulated crop context and free from pests and diseases from the soil.

By controlling environmental parameters, such as light, nutrients, temperature, pH, and conductivity, results are obtained much higher than traditional crops, without having to use pesticides that often produce harmful effects on the culture itself.

The hydroponic cultivation technique maximizes the yield in terms of quality, quantity, and speed. For this reason, hydroponic crops are becoming increasingly popular and appreciated not only by professionals and large distribution chains (we point out that most of the tomatoes on sale today in supermarkets come from hydroponics) both from small direct growers and - for pleasure or work - they decide to try their hand at crops of this type.

Chapter 2

HISTORY

"INVENTED BY THE BABYLONIANS AND THE AZTECS"

The hydroponic cultivation technique has deep roots in the history of humanity and arises from particular needs. In the 21st century, with the increase in specific needs, it is still topical. Indeed, interest is renewed today.

The first examples of soilless cultivation can be considered the hanging gardens of the Babylonians or the floating ones of the Aztecs of Mexico and the Chinese.

The Aztecs did not have arable land; for this, they implemented an ingenious system to use the existing lake in their territory. They built rafts of reeds and rushes tied together. On them, they placed fertile soil dredged from the bottom of the lakc and used it to grow different vegetables. These rafts were often connected and sometimes brought the gardener's home. The plants emitted the roots that headed towards the lake water. At the time of sale of the products, the raft was brought to the marketplace. This cultivation system was used until the 19th century.

More scientific forms of hydroculture began in the 17th century. The Englishman John Woodward (1699) is usually referred to as the first person to have raised plants in a nutrient solution.

Starting in the early 19th century, scholars began to understand that plants need nitrogen, potassium, phosphorus, calcium, sulfur, and iron. Later, around 1860, two German plant physiologists, Sachs and Knop, recognizing how difficult it was to qualitatively and quantitatively study the essential elements in plants grown in a medium as complex as the soil, cultivated plants with their roots immersed in a solution of salts. Minerals (a nutrient solution), whose chemical composition was controlled within limits set by the purity of the chemicals then available. Other researchers later showed that growth improved if the roots were aerated. However, these were practices restricted to laboratories and aimed at studying plant growth and nutrition.

In 1929, William Frederick Gericke, a plant physiologist from the University of California (Berkeley), proposed using water culture methods to produce cultivated plants on a commercial scale, rather than as a research tool. He called the technique "aquaculture." Gericke later in 1937, at the suggestion of Setchell of the University of California, announced that the method was to be called "hydroponics" since the term water-culture had previously been defined as the breeding of plants and aquatic animals.

Setchell called hydroponics "the art and science of crop production in a liquid culture medium." Hydroponics derives from the Greek hydro, which means water and ponos, which means work (literally water that works) and is analogous to the word "geoponics," the ancient term for agriculture. Other and new terms were coined later, such as "nutriculture" and "chemiculture," all indicating the principle illustrated above. In hydroponics, Gericke cultivated vegetables (chard, radish, carrot, potato, etc.), cereals, ornamental and fruit plants, as well as flowers. Using large tanks, he successfully bred tomato plants over 7m long in his laboratory.

In 1936 Gericke and Tavernetti showed that by heating the nutrient solution, it was possible to grow the tomato throughout the year and produce fruit for 8-9 months. They also stated that the potential yields of tomato grown in nutrient solutions were many times larger than those obtained on soil due to the higher density and height of the plants as well as the longer duration of the growing period

In the late 1930s, two of the leading scientists of the University of California, Hoagland, and Arnon, were commissioned to study hydroponics and, in 1938, published the bulletin on "nutriculture," a term that included all the methods for growing plants in a medium other than natural soil.

One of the first successes of hydroponics was in 1930 on the island of Wake, a rocky atoll in the Pacific, stopping point for transoceanic flights. On that island, the production of hydroponic vegetables was the only practical method of obtaining fresh vegetables for the passengers and crew of Pan America Airways. Fresh vegetables could not be shipped to the island of Wake, due to the high costs, and could not be bred because of the lack of land. Hydroponics represented an ideal solution.

Subsequently, this technology was used in some limited applications on the Atlantic and Pacific islands during the Second World War.

After the war, the University of Purdue spread hydroponics (called nutricolture) in a series of popular bulletins that described in detail the nutrient solutions for both liquid and aggregate systems (in solid medium).

Despite the commercial interest, these cultivation systems did not spread due to the high costs for the construction of the cultivation benches.

After about 20 years, interest in hydroponics was renewed thanks to the advent of plastics that were used not only in greenhouse covers but also in cultivation products. And they were also crucial for the introduction of drip irrigation.

Sericulture began to expand significantly in Europe and Asia during the 1950s and 1960s, and relevant hydroponic systems were experienced in California, Arizona, Abu Dhabi, and Iran in the 1970s. In these desert locations, the benefits of technology were motivated by the durability and advantage of solar radiation, which maximized photosynthetic production. Unfortunately, the oil crisis that began in 1973 increased the costs for heating and cooling controlled environment agriculture by 1-2 orders of magnitude. This, together with the few chemicals registered for the control of pathogens, caused more than one failure and diminished the interest in hydroponics, especially in the USA.

However, research on hydroponics has continued. In the late 1970s, researchers from the Glasshouse Crops Research Institute in Great Britain developed the nutrient film technique (NFT).

After 20 years, interest in soilless crops seems renewed both among researchers and among farmers, especially in areas where there is more significant concern about the pollution of groundwater caused by fertilizers and the use of chemicals for soil disinfection.

Today, although hydroponics is still a system little used with respect to the quantity of soil dedicated to protected crops, it is thought that, in the short term, it will find more space in the agricultural panorama since some problems will be solved such as:

- the need to reduce production costs;

- the need to improve production;

- the increase in environmental pollution linked to intensive agriculture and the legislative constraints deriving from it;

- the lack of resources such as water, work, energy.

Chapter 3

THE ADVANTAGES AND DISADVANTAGES OF HYDROPONIC CULTURES

Soilless cultivation is a useful tool for controlling crop growth and production through mineral nutrition management.

The main advantages to be registered are:

1. Shortening of development times.

Hydroponic crops should be used in artificially illuminated environments or greenhouses to keep environmental conditions under control.

Precisely the respect of the necessary ecological conditions allows us to speed up the growth of the plants and to achieve maturation in less time. However, the possibility of using these systems in outdoor cultivation is not excluded.

Plants in a hydroponic system develop faster than a traditional method in the ground as there are more considerable attention and greater control of nutrients as well as a more prosperous supply of oxygen to the root system. By breathing more easily, plants accelerate their metabolism and take less time to grow.

The shortening of development times leads to a reduction in the number of hours of light and, therefore, the switching on of the lamps and the operation of the extractors, with a consequent decrease in the expenditure of electricity and an extension of the life of the system. Furthermore, the shorter the cycle, the less likely it is that diseases will develop;

2. Better working conditions from plant to harvest, also with control of the actual crop needs;

3. Productivity per meter higher, thanks to a higher density of seedlings and the elimination of the attack by soil pathogens.

4. Increase in post-harvest product quality.

The vegetables produced in hydroponics do not contain the remains of chemicals used for geosterilization, they are cleaner, and from a nutritional point of view, they do not show any difference with the products cultivated on the soil.

Hydroponics is considered an eco-compatible cultivation technique as it does not involve geosterilization, and inclosed cycles, the use of water and fertilizers is reduced.

The quality of agricultural and horticultural products has also made remarkable progress: the market appreciates not only the traditional aspects (freshness, taste, and flavor) but also aspects such as production conditions (environmental and social responsibility) and product safety.

Although hydroponic crops offer a number of undoubted advantages, they are not free from some disadvantages. The price of a system for hydroponic cultivation is higher than a traditional one.

The environment used in addition to having a higher cost also implies a higher maintenance expense. In addition to this disadvantage, the cost of electricity used for light, and the circulation of water significantly affects the final gain.

Although the process is straightforward, a good knowledge of the plants that you want to grow and the nutrients that will be used throughout the process is required. Without an adequate understanding of the substances to be used, all the plants in cultivation will lead to death in a short time.

After careful consideration of the various pros and cons that hydroponic cultivation systems offer, you will be able to determine if this type of cultivation is right for you.

Obviously, if the pros outweigh the cons, then you can choose to use this process. On the other hand, if you see it as a risky choice, then perhaps it is better to choose a more conventional method for your crops.

In the end, hydroponics has always been considered an efficient solution for the production of vegetables and plants.

Chapter 4

TECHNIQUES FOR HYDROPONIC CULTIVATION

When planning hydroponic cultivation, various factors must be taken into consideration, such as the type of plant (e.g., tomatoes, strawberries, or salad), the place where it will be mounted (indoor cultivation or external greenhouse), the size of the system or the environment.

The above factors influence the choice of the type of technique to be used. Here are some of them, none is the best, but each one is perfect to use according to a specific situation.

4.1 Hydroponic cultivation technique in DWC

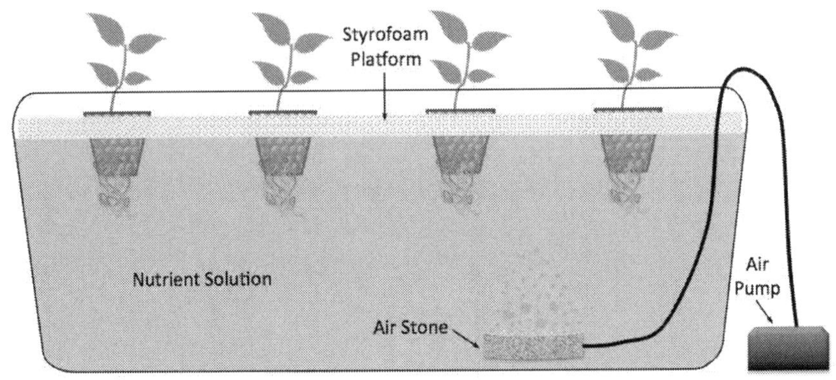

DWC, an acronym for Deep Water Culture, or deep water cultivation, is a hydroponic cultivation technique that consists of growing plants in a highly oxygenated solution based on water and fertilizers.

Compared to the other hydroponic cultivation methods, which use an inert substrate such as expanded clay, rock wool, perlite, etc. for radical propagation, in DWC the roots are completely (or almost) immersed within the solution that will do both substrates that act as a carrier for nutrients.

It is, therefore, possible to grow large plants with minimum use of the substrate, a fistful of expanded clay in which to make the young seedling take root and hold it till the roots coming out of the jar will be able to grow in the solution. For this reason, cultivation in deep water can be considered a middle ground between traditional hydroponics and aeroponics.

The advantages of growing in DWC can be summarized in:

-Accelerated growth, as the higher concentration of oxygen at the roots, stimulates the absorption of nutrients and the metabolism of the plant

-Increased production: plants grown in DWC have higher yields than those grown on land

-Minimum use of substratum: it will no longer be necessary to move large volumes of soil or other substrates as a.small amount of expanded clay is sufficient to grow large plants

-Little maintenance: there are no drips that could get clogged or water pumps that, in the event of a malfunction, would block the irrigation of the plants. Even in the event of a blackout, plants grown in DWC would survive.

Cultivation in deep water is best suited in those situations where the temperature can be controlled, in particular, that of the water; for this reason, they are well suited to be used indoors for the cultivation of medium or large plants. Instead, they are less suitable in very hot places, unless a solution refrigeration system such as a chiller is used.

A variant of the cultivation in deep water is the so-called floating systems, mainly used for the cultivation of salads. The plants are on boards that float inside a tank, and the roots grow immersed in the solution and are oxygenated by movement pumps or aerators.

4.2 Hydroponic cultivation technique NFT

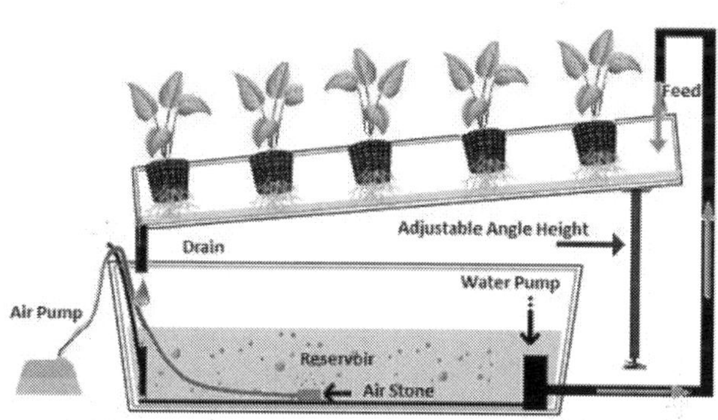

NFT, an acronym for Nutrient Film Technique, is based on the principle that the roots of the plant grow in contact with water that flows non-stop. In this way the roots themselves are non-stop enriched by the gaseous exchange with the oxygen present in the air and absorb the nutrients and oxygen present in the solution.

In general, these systems are made up of perforated conduits connected to a storage tank and a pump that continually keeps the solution circulating. It is crucial that the pump always works. In the event of a stop, the solution would cease to reach the roots, which could dry out in a few hours.

This system works very well with different types of plants, from salads to strawberries or larger plants, it is possible to adapt the size of the raceways and the distance of the holes, as well as the arrangement in the space in particular when you want to use it vertically.

4.3 Hydroponic cultivation technique in Dutch Bucket

It is a plastic bucket with a square or rectangular base, with a particular shape that allows it to be placed along a discharge line that leads to a storage tank. From this, the solution is distributed from above to each bucket through a pump. It irrigates the roots, and flows back through the drain channel.

In Dutch buckets, the roots of plants grow inside clay or perlite, materials with good draining power that allow a lot of air and, therefore, oxygen to pass through them.

Through drip trays, the plants receive the necessary water and nutrients. A siphon present at the bottom of each bucket ensures that a few centimeters of the solution are always available, which, in the event of a blackout, would be a reserve, giving the grower more time to intervene.

Another significant advantage is that they lend themselves to being assembled in a personalized way. It is possible to vary the distance between them, they can be arranged on different floors or to be easily moved from one place to another.

This system is reasonably easy to implement and lends itself very well to use in both home and commercial greenhouses.

4.4 Hydroponic cultivation technique on coconut coir

Coconut is a substrate with excellent characteristics for hydroponic cultivation. It has good water retention, protects the root system and at the same time offers a remarkable passage of air and therefore better oxygenation

The coconut fiber before being used for this purpose is washed and filtered, then dehydrated and compacted into blocks or slabs that make it convenient for storage.

Before being reused, these must be rehydrated; at this point, the fiber will absorb the water, increasing in volume up to 5 times.

Being an inert substrate, therefore devoid of nutrients, these must be supplied through a nutrient solution, which will be administered at intervals through drippers with a series of daily cycles.

Another significant advantage is the possibility of being reused and being able to grow for 2 or 3 cycles with the same substrate.

The coconut plates are suitable for the cultivation of all plants, and in particular, they are trendy in the cultivation of strawberries. The slabs can be arranged on raceways or overhead supports that make the cultivator's job more comfortable as well as harvesting.

4.5 Kratky method

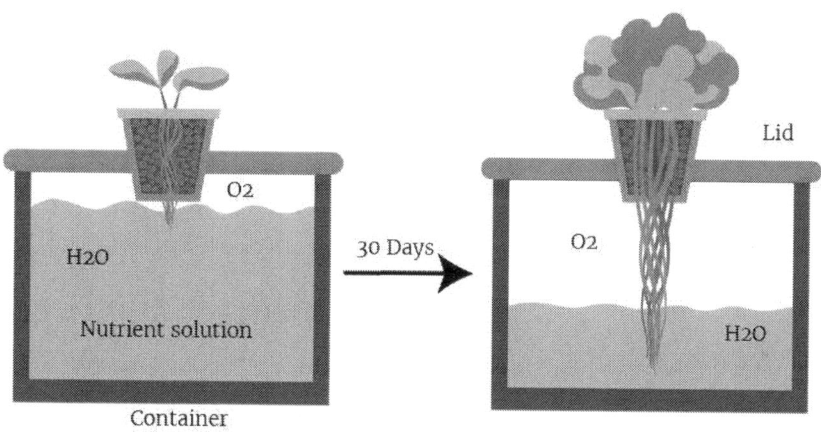

The first system we recommend for creating a hydroponic garden is the famous Kratky method. It is undoubtedly one of the simplest, suitable for those approaching Hydroponics for the first time and is ideal for those who want to grow vegetables.

With this system, you can grow vegetables such as lettuce and spinach. It is also a system suitable for growing tomatoes.

For its realization, the following materials are needed:

- a mason jar, container, or bucket;

- seed starter cubes;

- growing medium (Hydroton works well);

- Net Pots;

- PH kit.

These elements allow you to configure a passive system, which does not require electricity and which can operate for several weeks without maintenance.

That's it, other than water and nutrients.

First, you should have a seedling ready. The seedling can be cultivated in a seed starter cube. The roots should start to become visible on the bottom of the cube before transplanting.

You can only use one plant per seed starting cube and one per net pot.

You can grow all kinds of plants using the Kratky method, from tomatoes to lettuce. You need a three to five-gallon bucket for tomatoes or cucumbers and a mason jar or a plastic soda bottle for lettuce. I advise using wide mouth mason jars with 3-inch net pots.

The Kratky method is a set and forget growing method you can use on your windowsill. Once the plant starts to grow, the level in the container will drop. As the roots grow, they will keep up with the lowering water level. This will continue until the plant is fully grown. Lettuce needs around sixteen fluid ounces (four hundred and seventy-five milliliters), while the three to five-gallon (eleven to eighteen liter) bucket for tomatoes needs to be refilled often.

The roots will take up the water, and the plant will start to grow. The nutrient solution will drain, but the roots will keep up with the draining water level.

The empty space that is created will provide the roots with oxygen. This will continue until the plant is fully matured, and the water has drained. You need to aim for the plant growth to keep up with the water in the reservoir.

You need to place the setup in a well-lit environment. You must darken the outside of the container with tin foil. This is to discourage algae from growing in the container. Do not use black paper or paint because it will heat the water in the box.

If the water has entirely drained while your plant is not fully grown yet, you need to top-up the water. You need to fill it up halfway, so only half of the roots are submerged.

This system can be established virtually anywhere and needs very little space. I recommend trying this setup for everyone who is starting with Hydroponics.

Build the system

Smaller plants:

Take a two or three-inch net pot and put some Hydroton at the bottom. Place your seedling with the seed starter cube in the net pot. Fill the sides with Hydroton for the cube to stay upright. Fill the nutrient solution in the container until it touches the bottom of the seed starting cube. Darken the water container so no algae will grow inside.

Bigger plants:

Use a three or five-gallon bucket and use a six-inch net pot with a lid. The process is the same as the smaller plant. The six-inch net pot will be more natural for the plant to hold onto because the root system will be much more significant.

If you refill the bucket, only fill it up halfway. This is for the roots to access oxygen. If you were to submerge the whole root system, root rot would occur, and your plant will die.

4.6 Wick system

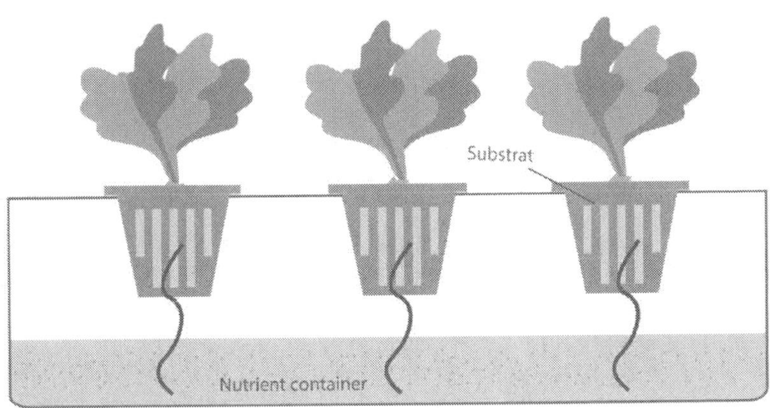

Simple, passive Hydroponic system.

The wick system is another easy system to make hydroponic growth.

It doesn't have any moving parts, and there is no reliance on electricity.

The plant is cultured in a substratum, which is supplied with a nutrient solution by the capillary action of the wick.

This is a straightforward system to build and one that will give you a great introduction to Hydroponics. It's very similar to the Kratky method but with the addition of a wick.

You will need:

- a plastic bottle or tub with lid;

- two-inch net pots;

- seed starter cube;

- growing media of your choice;

- wicking rope.

Building the Wick system

The water container has the water and nutrients a plant needs. Above this sits the plant and a wicking rope that will bring water and nutrients to the plant using the capillary action of the wick.

Start by drilling two-inch holes in the top of your lid. Drill as many as you need to fill the top of the lid. Don't forget that your seedlings will grow, so take that into account. Lettuce, for example, should be six to eight inches apart from each other (center to center) depending on the variety.

Start by filling your container with water and nutrient solution.

Take the two-inch net pots and put the wicking rope trough, so it touches the grow media. Make sure it will touch the roots of the seedling you are going to put in.

Place the lid on the container and place the net cups into the holes you drilled. The wick will be inside the water solution. If done correctly, the wick will deliver the nutrient-rich water to the plant roots. Make this wick touch the bottom of the water reservoir. As the water slowly drains, the wick will provide water to the roots.

This is a good system for slightly smaller plants, such as lettuce and herbs. However, it is not very practical for more substantial plants like tomatoes, fruiting plants, and peppers. These tend to need an abundant supply of water and nutrients. The wick system may not be able to deliver them fast enough.

If you choose to create a wick system, you need to consider the right wick material carefully. It is worth testing a few and always soak them first to ensure they provide the most effective wicking action possible.

The best option found is using a thick candlewick. They are designed to wick up wax and are made of cotton. They are quite thick too. A roll of six feet will cost you $6. You can reuse these also.

You can make the reservoir as large as you like and increase the number of plants you have accordingly.

It is also important to underline that the wick will absorb water and nutrients evenly, but your plant may not. If the air is warmer than usual, the plant will evaporate more water than when it's colder. The evaporation will lead to water being drawn from the wick without the nutrients.

This can result in a build-up of nutrients on the wick, which will damage the ability of the wick to work effectively. Therefore, you should wash or rinse your wick after every harvest to remove excess nutrients (nutrient build-up).

Make sure you block the sun or your grow light from entering the water container. Wrap something around it for the light not to penetrate the container and create algae in the nutrient-rich water. Tinfoil is perfect for this. Avoid using black spray paint is it will heat the water in the box.

Alternative with a bottle

If you want an even easier method, you can use a plastic bottle and cut off the top. Flip the top of the bottle inside the base and place the wicking rope together with the wicking grow media inside. You can choose to leave the cap on and drill a hole in it or remove the cap entirely. You need to keep an eye on the reservoir as it will drain quickly.

Wick system disadvantages

The supply of the plants the wick is not as valid as with other hydroponic systems. The wick can become obstructed by mineral deposits. The problem of this system is that no extra oxygen is supplied to the roots. The system is technically simple, but plant growth is slower compared to other active hydroponic systems.

4.7 Ebb and Flow

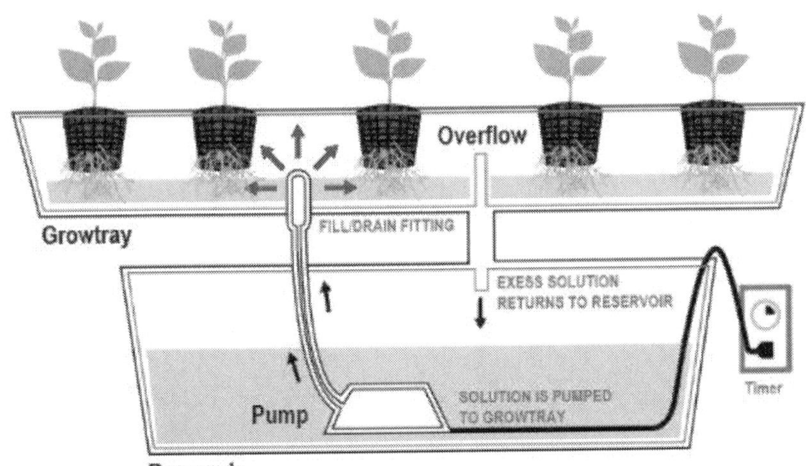

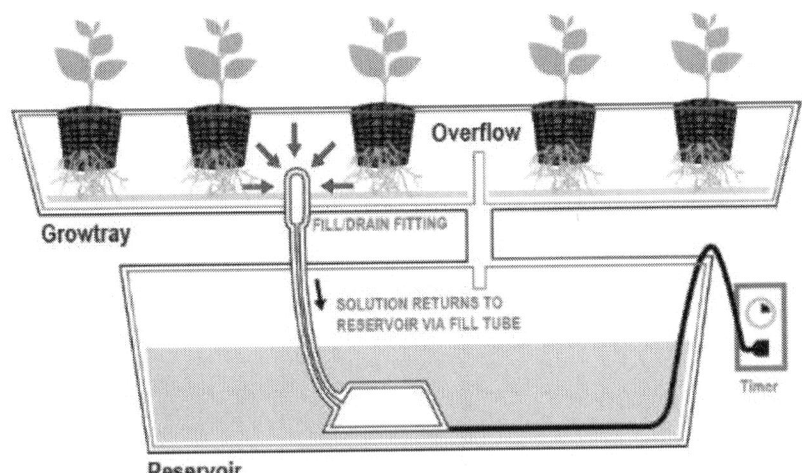

This is another system that's easy to set up, and it is mostly used for starting seeds.

As your experience with Hydroponics grows, you'll probably continue to start seeds with this system and then transplant them to a different setup. Commercial farms use this technique for their seedlings.

The Ebb and Flow system work by flooding, for a short time, the tray containing the substrate with a nutrient solution and then sending it back into the tank.

This action usually takes place with a submersible pump connected to a timer.

When the timer turns on the pump, the nutrient solution is pumped into the growth tray. When the timer switches off, the nutrient solution pump flows back into the tank.

The timer is set to switch on several times a day, depending on the size and type of plants, temperature, humidity, and the kind of substrate used.

Ebb and flow system works with a variety of substrates. The interior of the growth tray can be filled with cultivation rocks, gravel, or flaky Rockwool. Many people like to use individual pots full of a substrate. This makes it easier to move plants around or even move them in or out of the system.

The main disadvantage of this type of system is that some kinds of culture mediums (gravel, Growrocks, Perlite) can create multiple drawbacks, such as power outages and pump or timer faults. In that case, the roots can dry out quickly if the irrigation cycles are interrupted.

This problem can be alleviated by using cultivation substrates that retain more water, such as Rockwool, vermiculite, or coconut fiber.

Building your Ebb and Flow System

Here that you'll need:

- a container for your plants

- a water reservoir

- a pump, preferably submersible

- a timer for the pump

- tubing for the pump

- a siphon of your choice

- your choice of growing medium

Start by drilling two holes in the base of your plant container. One hole is for the water to be delivered to the tray; the other will act as an overflow.

Add your water and nutrients to the water container and turn on your pump. You can time how long it takes to fill the plant container until it overflows.

When you shut the pump off, the water will drain back down through the pump pipe and into the water container, creating the ebb and flow.

Probably the sunlight or artificial light will get to the water in the flood and drain tray, and you will need to clean out algae regularly to ensure it isn't using the nutrients and dissolved oxygen meant for the plants.

4.8 Drip system

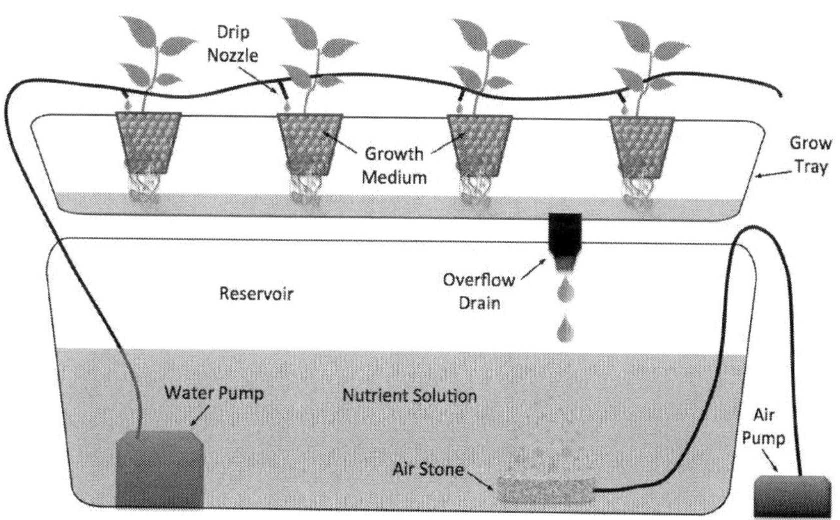

You may have already come across a drip system with conventional soil-potted plants. This is a popular option because it is elementary to add or remove plants and automate the system.

The principle behind this type of hydroponics system is to get the nutrient-rich water to the roots, by dripping it slowly onto the plant roots.

There are two methods of drip systems:

-recirculating

-non-recirculating

Most drip systems are designed as recirculating. A recirculating system pumps the water from the reservoir to the plants. It has a drainage system that allows the water to drain back into the reservoir, effectively allowing the water to go in a circle.

This is an efficient approach as water loss is minimized, only that which transpires from the plants or evaporates into the atmosphere is lost. You'll need a minimal amount of water to top up the system.

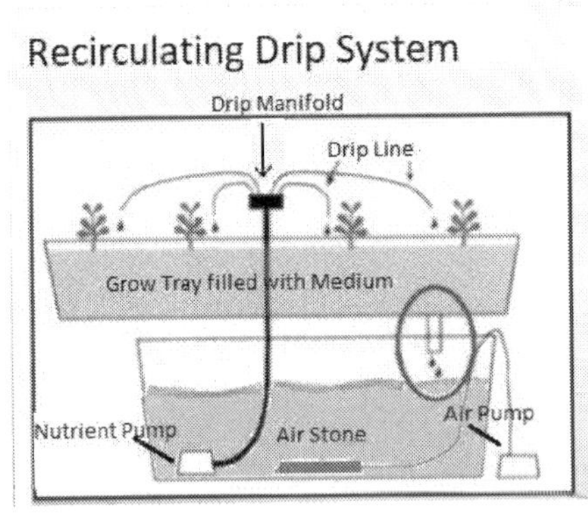

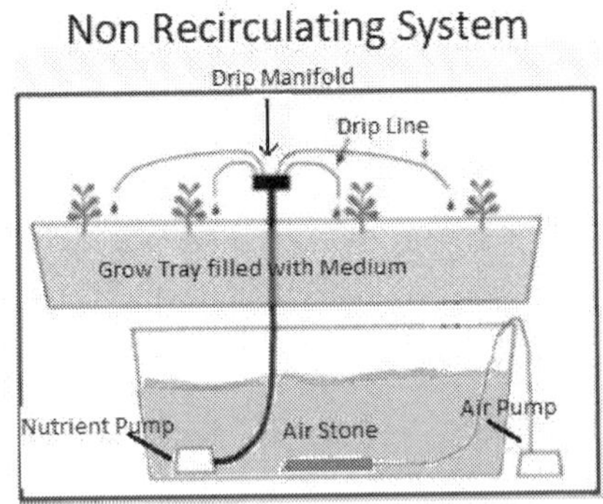

In contrast, the non-recirculating system doesn't allow the water to return to the reservoir. This is why they are also known as "run to waste" systems.

This may seem like a wasteful option as the water will need to be replenished regularly. However, this is a very popular option for commercial farmers because the costs involved are low.

The non-recirculating system is run with a top-up reservoir. The delivery of nutrient-rich water is carefully measured, so no water and nutrients are lost. This minimizes waste.

You will have to mix another batch with a predetermined ratio of nutrients and water. This makes the non-recirculating system easy to operate.

4.9 Vertical system

The vertical hydroponics system is a great space saver and can be made in many different forms. The vertical A system uses NFT channels for the plants while the vertical towers use custom grow towers or three-inch PVC pipes. Both use drip irrigation.

The A-frame hydroponic system is an excellent example of how to create a vertical garden that maximizes the number of plants that can develop in a small space without the need for soil.

This is something that could be done on a small scale, making it ideal for those who want to grow their food but lack the space to do it. Or it could easily be scaled up to a much larger system.

Another option worth considering is hydroponic towers.

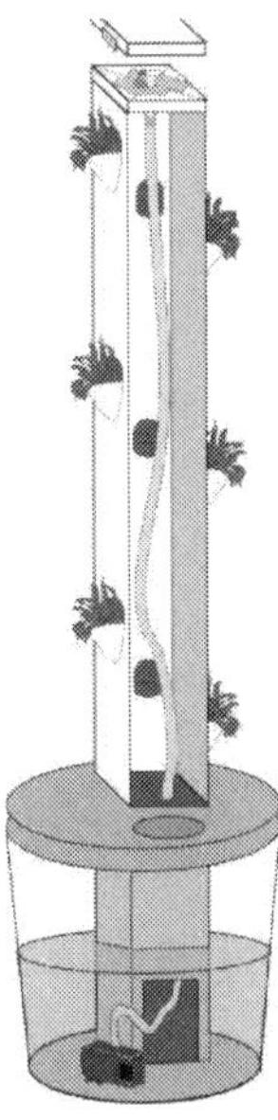

These hydroponic systems for vertical cultivation are ideal for those who have little space and do not have the opportunity to carve out a space for the creation of a traditional horizontal vegetable garden.

Directly related to your budget and the space you have available, you can decide how many towers you want.

A seven-foot tube has slots for approximately twenty plants. Therefore, if you start with six tubes, you will have enough space to grow one hundred and twenty plants.

The water will be supplied to the top of the grow towers and will drip into a collection gutter back to the reservoir.

These towers can be placed in a small greenhouse, in a garden, in a garage, or even in a small room in the house; more and more people are turning to vertical crops, both to experiment with new types of agriculture and for space needs.

4.10 Fogponics

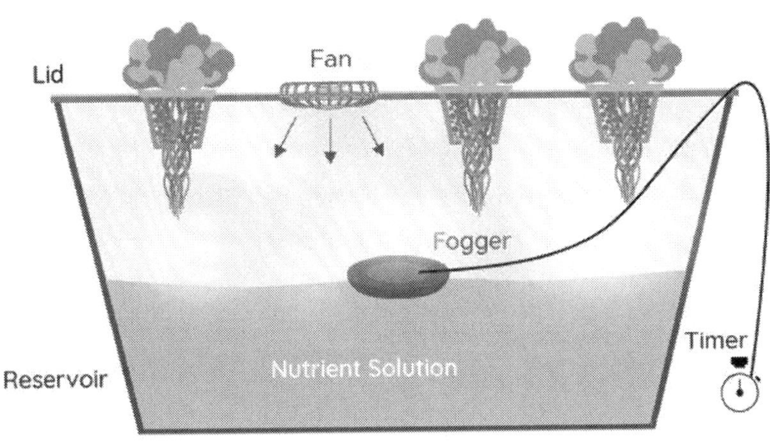

Fogponics works similarly to Aeroponics (that we'll talk about later in the book) but is an advanced form of these because this type of system uses fog instead of misting as the primary growing environment.

It is mainly used to create clones. The fog is created by an ultrasonic device that floats on the water. The vibration evaporates the water.

Fogponics or fog, and ponics (labor) can be defined as working fog. In its most straightforward meaning, in the Fogponics system, growers use the fog to grow plants.

The Fogponic method uses electric nebulizers to pump and vibrate. The combination of water and nutrients turns into humidity. The roots of the plants are, therefore, systematically enveloped by the humid and nutrient-filled mist that is created.

With this cultivation method, the tiny mist particles disperse and spread and completely impregnate the roots of the plants. Plants absorb all the nutrients they need together with moisture and oxygen, just like in all the active hydroponic cultivation methods we've talked about so far.

They don't have to "worry" about finding them in the ground, and therefore, every effort is made to grow, blossom, and germinate if it is a question of seedlings; in case we are producing clones, to root development.

There is a difference with the usual hydroponic systems: instead of taking oxygen from the water (in which an air pump is active), plants are suspended in the air.

In this way, their roots are easily wrapped in oxygen. Nebulizers supply water to plants, and a timer usually automates the action.

Fogponics operates just like Aeroponics. But are used the foggers instead of the water mist. They produce and atomize much smaller droplets than in Aeroponics, usually less than 10 microns in size.

In Fogponics, which plants are better?

Although, in principle, with Fogponics, we can grow all plants, it is advisable to focus on suitable plants to obtain the best results.

Seedling, clonings

The Fogponics system works very well with small plants and cloning. The little clones that have just been obtained from a cutting have poorly developed roots, and it is therefore rather difficult to make them absorb nutrients and keep them hydrated. At the same time, we should not exaggerate the amount of water; too much could excessively load the cloning, too little on the contrary will not give birth to the shoots or dry the roots.

The growers make available to their small clones a set of nutrients and humidity at controlled quantities through the fog produced in the Fogponics system.

Green vegs

The Fogponics also works best with green vegs, including lettuces, spinaches, kales, cucumbers, and beans.

Herbs

Most herbs like basil, mint, and chives thrive in the Fogponic system as it is lightweight, and have a short growing life span.

Advantages of Fogponics system

- Tiny sized droplets. The small droplets tend not to impinge on roots. The cuttings and little seedlings are very delicate and weak; the low-pressure fog does not harm them; that's why Fogponics works so well with cloning.

- High nutrient concentration. The high density of nutrients remains constant inside the tank.

- Easy to clean

Disadvantages of Fogponics system

- Heating produced by the atomizer

The atomizer will be turned on non-stop and can, therefore, increase the temperature inside the tank. The high temperature will evaporate the fog, and the roots can dry out. It will, therefore, be advisable to lower the temperature by programming a timer that will turn the foggers on and off. There is an alternative method: you can add ices. Or buy a water chiller.

- Built-up salt

Over time, the salt will accumulate in the system, and this will block the foggers. It will, therefore, be necessary to clean the system regularly. You can use a toothbrush or soak them all in vinegar. This will ensure that fogponics will always work best.

- Susceptible to a power outage

The whole Fogponics system works thanks to electricity. And the roots are not immersed in water, as in other hydroponic methods, but hung freely. If electricity is missing, the fog stops. All our plants will not be able to absorb the necessary moisture and nutrients; they will dry out quickly and could die.

- High initial cost

This advanced form of Hydroponics will cost you some start-up costs in the beginning.

4.11 Conclusions

There is, therefore, no perfect system or better than others, depending on their needs and experience, each grower will find one system more functional than another.

It is essential to carefully evaluate the various aspects that can influence the choice of the system and to fully understand which technique will be able to best express the potential of your hydroponic garden.

Chapter 5

STARTING CULTIVATION WITH HYDROPONIC TECHNIQUE

5.1 Necessary to Start Hydroponic Cultivation

Here the tools needed in the three germination, growth and final flowering stages

For the Germination Phase:

Necessary:

-Greenhouse (in which to germinate the seeds)

-Rockwool rock wool cubes (at least 1 for each seed to be germinated)

-Root Stimulator

Optional:

-Neon light

-Watertight heating resistance (allows to keep the temperature of the greenhouse stable at the optimal temperature of about 26 degrees)

For the growth and flowering phase:

Necessary:

-Indoor Lighting Kit (in chapter 5.4 we will explain how to choose the lighting system)

-Bulb / bulb

-Power supply

-Lamp / Reflector Holder

-Hydroponic system

-Expanded clay

-pH Tester

-EC Tester

-PH corrector

-Nourishments for the growth phase

-Nourishments for the flowering phase

-Timer for timing

Optional:

-Thermometer/hygrometer

-Grow box / Grow Room or Mylar tent

-Hop on and off (easy roller)

-Humidifier

-Cooling fan

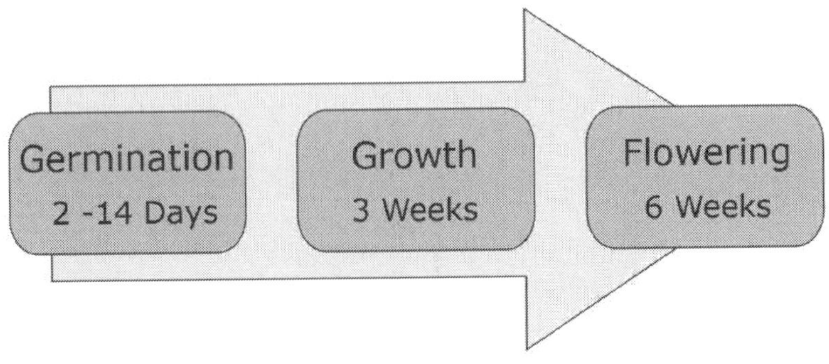

Indicative costs to be faced with starting Hydroponic cultivation at home or in a greenhouse

Establishing the final and exact cost of a plant dedicated to hydroponic cultivation is not that simple, because there are a series of variables that affect the ultimate price. However, it is possible to have a general idea to be able to orient yourself. For a private individual who wishes to start hydroponic cultivation at home, the cost to be incurred - for a basic starter kit - ranges between $450 and $550. At the same time, if you want a more complex system, using the latest products and highly technological products in terms of lamps, boxes, and extractors, it can reach $1.100/$1.200.

For those who wish, however, to start real hydroponic agriculture at a professional level, the costs vary significantly, due to a higher number of factors to consider in setting up the system.

Even in this case, however, it is possible to give an idea: it ranges from a minimum of $200 up to a maximum of $1.000, but of course, it is necessary to consider that these are indicative price ranges and that - in any case - the more the area of the cultivated greenhouse increases, the more the average cost will drop.

5.2 Preparation of the germination area

Prepare the rock wool cubes for germination

To prepare the germination area, it is necessary to have rock wool cubes and the root booster to develop the root system of the plants quickly. Below we illustrate the procedure to start the seed germination phase.

- Prepare a solution with 5 liters of water and 20 ml of root stimulator.

- Take the Rockwool cubes and leave them to soak for about 24 hours in the solution of water and Rootbooster to make the Rockwool cubes less alkaline (their pH tends to 7.0).

- The next day drains the cubes. Rockwool cubes retain a lot of water, so it is useful to drain the Rockwool cube to allow a correct exchange of water and oxygen.

- Insert the seed into the hole of the Rockwool cube at a depth of 1/2 (half) cm.

- Insert the cubes inside the mini-greenhouse and keep the temperature at about 79 °F (26 °C) with a high humidity rate (about 80%).

- Move the neon lamp closer and keep it on 24 hours a day.

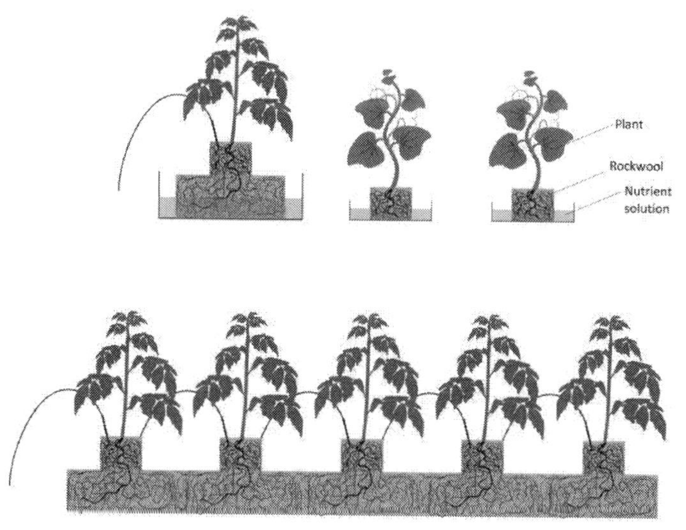

The seed does not initially need light. Once the seedling comes out of the Rockwool cube, however, it is essential to light it with delicate light (preferably neon) or HPS and/or MH lamp (monitoring temperature and humidity).

Seedlings that do not receive adequate light tend to have a very long stem. Depending on the type, quality, and age of the seeds, germination can take from 2 to 14 days.

The roots once crossed the Rockwool cube will tend to come out from the sides and from the bottom of the cube itself

N.B.: the seed in the germination phase is very delicate and must not be touched.

5.3 Installation of the Hydroponic System and Sprout Housing

Once the seed has germinated, it is necessary to plan the preparation of the hydroponic system to plant the rock wool cube.

But how does the hydroponic system work?

In fact, it is good to specify that there are many hydroponic systems on the market, with different characteristics.

In our example, we will use the Atami Wilma Large 4-bowl hydroponic system, which is one of the best-selling with a technology proven by historical results and now guaranteed.

If you decide to use other methods, you should always refer to the instruction manual provided by the manufacturer.

How does a Hydroponic system work and how to set it up?

Here is what we must foresee and prepare and how it is appropriate to set up - in detail - the hydroponic system.

-prepare the lower tank;

-place the pump in the tank;

-house the upper tank;

-place the vases on the upper tank;

-connect the pump to the main fitting;

-connect the main pipe to the drippers and support rods;

-fill the expanded clay pots (remember to wash the clay thoroughly to eliminate dust and impurities)

-connect the pump to the timer and to the power supply (in chapter 5.6 we will deal with the timing of the hydroponic system);

-fill the tank with water and fertilizers (in section 5.11 we will deal in-depth with this topic)

-house the rock wool cube containing the sprout inside the vase containing the expanded clay and house the drippers so that they supply water directly on the cube.

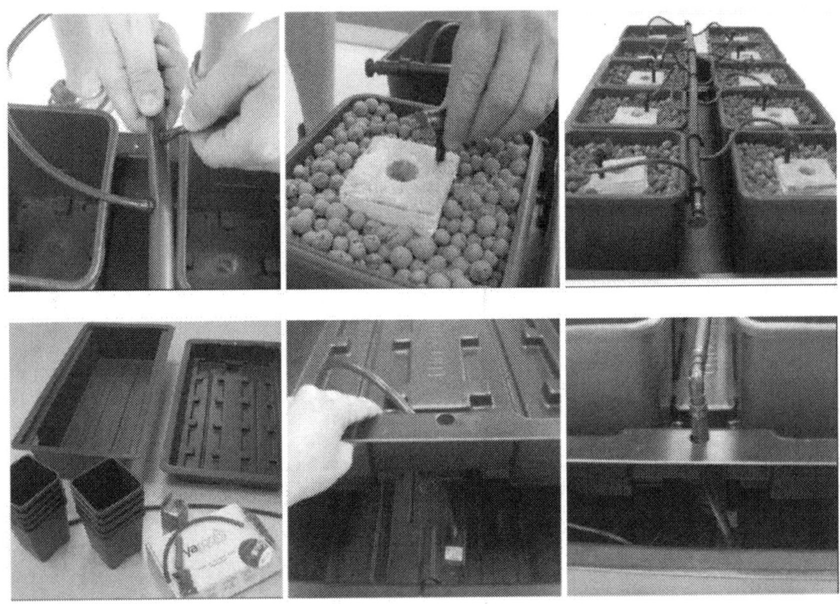

5.4 The lighting system

Once the cubes containing the sprouts have been placed inside the hydroponic system, we must begin to illuminate the seedling (and this applies both to indoor cultivation in the ground, both for hydroponic cultivation, and obviously for aeroponics). To do this, we must prepare a suitable lighting system capable of making the sprout grow and flourish by simulating the effect of sunlight.

A lighting system for hydroponics and indoors is composed of the following elements:

Power supply (or Ballast)

It is used to provide a discharge of current sufficient to turn on the lamp. There are two types of power supplies on the market, the iron-magnetic and the electronic ones.

Electronic ballasts have the advantage over ferromagnetic ballasts of:

-consume less electricity;

-to heat very little;

-to be more stable and therefore increase the life of the bulb;

-wiring is more straightforward because they have the connection to the electrical network already wired;

-some models (dimmable) can adjust the watts and, therefore, to manage bulbs of different wattage.

Hydroponic lamp: what is it?

The lamp that in indoor and hydroponic cultivation provides a specific light spectrum to simulate the effect of the sun.

We often speak of a hydroponic lamp, but - in reality - it is more appropriate to speak of a specific bulb or bulb for hydroponic cultivation, which - thanks to the particular spectrum of light - simulates and reproduces the effects and benefits of sunlight. There are various types of bulbs on the market dedicated to indoor cultivation. The difference lies in the kind of technology and the different background of light and colors. For growth, a blue light spectrum is suggested.

For the flowering phase, however, an illumination spectrum tending towards orange/red is indicated. Agro lamps are usable during the growth and flowering periods, while MH is usable only during the vegetative phase (when the plant grows) while HPS is for the flowering stage.

The choice between Agro and MH - HPS: Agro bulbs are certainly a more comfortable and economical solution than MH and HPS bulbs since they are used throughout the life cycle of the plant.

Agro lamps have the disadvantage of having a lower yield during the growth phase compared to MH.

Lamp holder / Reflector

It is used to accommodate the bulb and spread the light distribution in the cultivation area.

Also, in this case, there are many models on the market and properties. We can say, however, that there are two basic types of reflectors, air-cooled reflectors and those that are not. The latter has the advantage of being designed in such a way as to allow forced air passage from an extractor that can cool the heat emitted by the bulb, effectively preventing the temperature from rising inside the grow room.

Choose the size of the indoor and hydroponic lighting system

The diagram below helps you to define the size of the lighting system, starting from the available space and the number of plants you wish to grow. The size of the grow box (optional) to be associated with the type of lighting system is also indicated for convenience.

Warning! Always remember that the power supply and the bulb must have the same wattage

	150 watt	250 watt	400 watt	600 watt	1.000 watt
number of plants	1/2	2/4	3/6	4/10	8/18
Square meters	0,5	0,75	1	1,4	1,5
Grow Room Box	32"x32"x72"	36"x36"x72"	39"x39"x80"	48"x48"x80"	96"x48"x80"
	70x70x180 cm	80x80x180 cm	100x100x200 cm	120x120x200 cm	240x120x200 cm

Lighting system wiring:

1. Connect the power supply to the mains *

There are various types of power supplies on the market.

Some are simpler to wire such as electronic ballasts because they already have a connection to the electricity grid ready, others like ferromagnetic ones are more complex

2. Connect the power supply to the lamp/reflector holder *

3. The current from the power supply must be brought and connected to the lamp holder to which the lamp is screwed and then powered.

The lamp holder for these types of uses always has a standard attachment called E40.

4. The lamp/reflector holder: It has the function of reflecting and diffusing the light produced by the lamp. Generally, it is supplied complete with a lamp holder.

There are various shapes and sizes on the market. It is often provided with protective plastics, so it is good to be careful and remove them before putting it into operation.

5. Screw the bulb to the bulb holder *.

6. Once everything is wired, screw the bulb to the lamp holder until it stops. Clean the bulb with a cloth before turning it on.

* Refer to the manuals and instructions provided by the manufacturer for the connections between the parts.

5.5 Set up the Grow Room

The optimal environmental conditions in which to set up the cultivation area

A grow room is a growing area for indoor growing. It is possible to grow indoors in any closed space. However, it is necessary to take into account several factors to ensure that all the parameters useful for the growth of the plant are regularly monitored and controlled to obtain the best possible result.

Below we can list the essential elements to manage in the cultivation area (grow room):

1. The light

2. The temperature

3. Humidity

4. Aeration, ventilation and carbon dioxide (CO2)

In the following chapters, we will deal in-depth with each of these points and analyze the solutions to the most common problems that occur when the threshold values of each parameter are exceeded.

In the image, you will find an illustration of all the components useful for managing vital signs in a grow room.

GROW ROOM SETUP

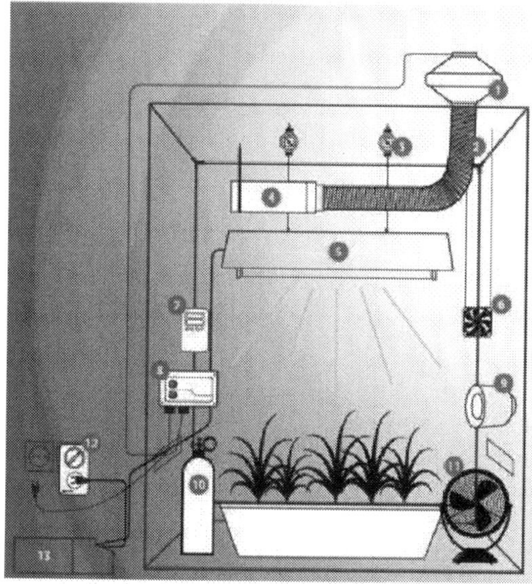

1) Air extractor
Needed to control temperature and humidity

2) Flexible conduct
Connect the extractor to the carbon filter

3) Easy Roller
Pulleys to adjust the height of the lamp

4) Activated carbon filter
Filters the air exiting the air extractor making it odor-free

5) Lamp

6) Axial fan
Eliminates "hotspot" produced by the lamp

7) Hygrometer
Measures the values of min/max temperature and humidity

8) Climate control unit
Connected to the extractor, it manages the temperature and humidity

9) Axial extractor
Introduces air flow

10) Co2 cylinder

11) Cooling fan
Avoids stagnation of air in the cultivation environment

12) Analog timer
Daily timer to manage the light

13) Hps Mh power supply
Able to turn on bulbs Hps, Mh and Agro

5.6 The Light in the Grow Room

Light in indoor cultivation is an essential element. Plants will need to receive the right amount of light from recreating the cycle that naturally provides the sun in outdoor cultivation.

In indoor cultivation, it is advisable to completely isolate the cultivation area, perhaps by purchasing a grow box that prevents access to natural light so that we can artificially control the hours of light and dark.

Another advantage of the ready-made grow rooms that can be purchased on the market is that they are lined with reflective material, which guarantees complete reflexivity, which allows better light diffusion. If a grow room is not used, it is possible to cover the cultivation area with reflective sheets.

Light hours in the growth and flowering stages

During the growth phase, it is necessary to provide the plant with about 18 hours of light per day.

In the third or fourth week of the growth phase, it is possible to reduce the hours of light from 18 to 12. The plant will perceive the arrival of autumn (effect: "shorter days"), then it will begin to bloom before winter arrives.

In any case, it is not recommended to make the plant bloom when it is still too small and weak since it would not be able to support many flowers.

Using the timer to control the switching on and off of the lights

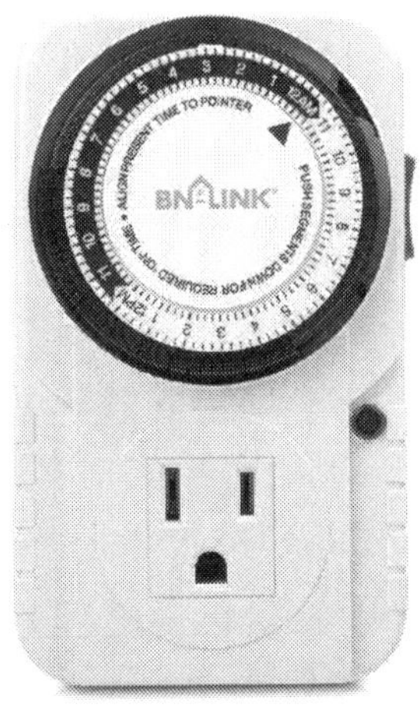

The timer is handy for regulating the switching on and off of the lights. There are several types on the market; the cheapest ones are the analog timers that provide programming in 24 hours in general in a 15-minute passage.

The digital timers are set to multiple programming and arranged to set up to 20 different programs. Finally, there are timers and multiple channels that lend light to the various power outlets.

5.7 Temperature in the Grow Room

The tools to control and regulate the temperature in Hydroponic cultivation

In all indoor and outdoor cultivations, regardless of the type of soil or substrate used and the type of systems used to grow plants, temperature plays a fundamental role in the success of cultivation, even in indoor ones with a hydroponic system. For this reason, it is one of the parameters to be monitored continuously and adjusted, to make sure that it is always in the preset and therefore optimal parameters, which oscillate between 70°F (21°C) and 82°F (28°C) degrees centigrade. If the temperature rises above 82°F (28°C) or drops below 70°F (21°C), it could cause severe damage to your plants.

To prevent this from happening, it is essential to monitor using specific measuring instruments, i.e., thermometers and thermo-hygrometers.

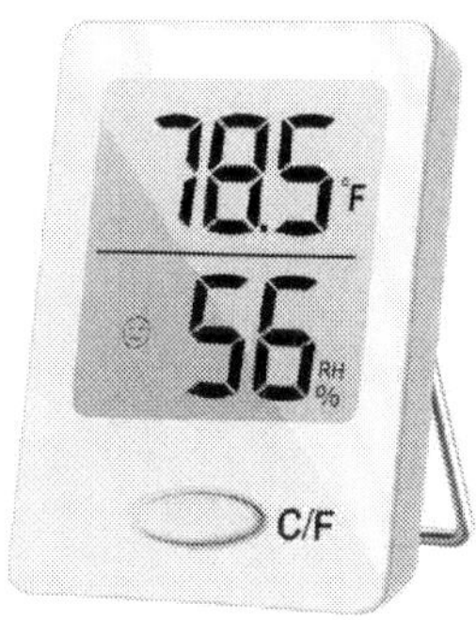

The recommendation is to buy a digital thermometer that allows you to correctly and accurately check the temperature of the grow room or hydroponic cultivation environment, at any time of the day, including monitoring and recording the minimum and maximum temperature reached during an arc of time.

Only in this way can we notice if the temperature has exceeded the recommended parameters and avoid problems that could be more or less serious.

But what should be done if the temperature rises or falls compared to the recommended values? How is it possible to run for cover?

To lower the temperature in the grow room of your hydroponic cultivation, it is possible to use an aspirator or air extractor, which sucks in and extracts the hot air, gradually lowering the room temperature. If the rise in temperature should occur often, it is possible to provide a thermostat programmed to activate the extractor only during the hot hours, when the indoor lights are on. If the temperature does not drop even with the extractor, an air conditioner can be used to lower it.

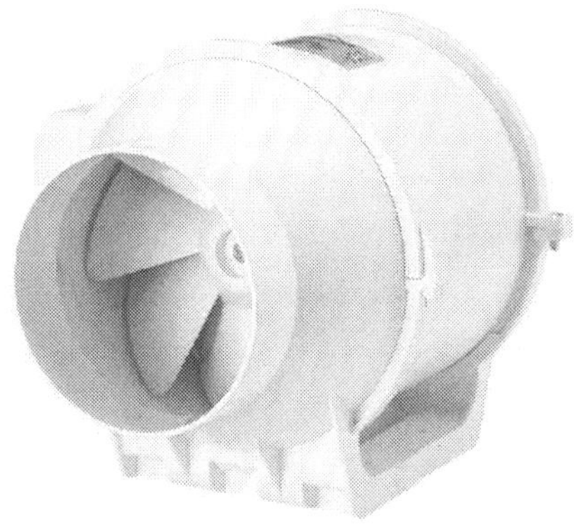

If, on the contrary, the temperature of indoor cultivation with hydroponic system should be too low, below 21 degrees centigrade, it is possible - even in this case - to use a thermostat, which can activate a stove capable of heating the environment and raise the temperature by a few degrees, especially when the lights are off.

5.8 Grow Room moisture

Humidity is another fundamental parameter to be kept under control in the indoor cultivation area. The ideal humidity for indoor growing is around 50-60%. The hygrometer is the measuring instrument to monitor the percentage of humidity present in the grow room. When the humidity is too high, it causes molds to arise, which results in the progressive deterioration of the plant.

What to do if the humidity is too high:

To decrease the humidity in the grow room, an air extractor is sufficient as for the temperature. The suction of hot and humid air allows a lowering of humidity.

What to do if the humidity is too low:

When the humidity is too low, a humidifier is sufficient for a grow room.

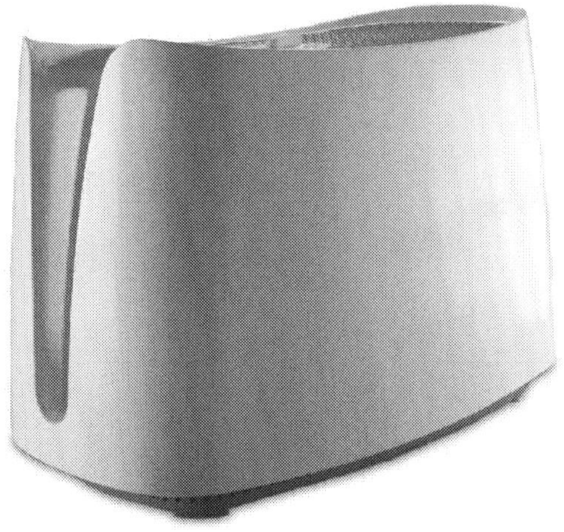

5.9 The Ventilation of the Grow Room

Proper ventilation allows our cultivation air to avoid humidity accumulation and temperature rise.

The ventilation in the grow room, and in general, the air circulation is a factor of primary importance. As previously seen, proper ventilation allows our cultivation air to avoid the accumulation of humidity and raising the temperature.

The air extraction process, therefore, becomes an indispensable element whose goal is the extraction of internal air so that all the air is extracted every 4/6 minutes. An extraction system consists of the following items:

1. The extractor to suck the air

2. The duct or extraction hose

3. The fan for the intake of fresh air

4. A fan (optional to improve air recirculation)

5. An activated carbon filter (optional to eliminate odors at the outlet)

Selection and sizing of the ventilation system.

An air extractor must be chosen above all based on the flow rate. To calculate it, multiply the volume of the grow room (or grow box) by 75. To choose the appropriate extractor, do this calculation:

Height x Width x Depth x 75 = Air extractor flow rate.

Once the extractor flow rate has been calculated, we can choose a suitable model. Once the model and its diameter have been selected, the pipes must be purchased, paying attention to respect their diameter or choosing the necessary reducers.

To join the extractor to the pipe/duct, use jointing bands or resistant scotch tape.

It is possible to automate the ventilation circuit through special control units which have the function of regulating the extractor power when parameters (temperature and humidity) vary.

Carbon dioxide (CO_2) in the Grow Room

When growing in an enclosed environment, there is a risk that the growing plants consume a lot of carbon dioxide (CO_2); if this occurs, the growth of the plant will slow down significantly.

To maintain high levels of Co2, it will be sufficient to let outside air into the grow room through an extractor. Often, however, excessive air circulation causes the temperature to drop excessively. In this case, we can forcefully dispense carbon dioxide through a CO_2 bottle dispenser.

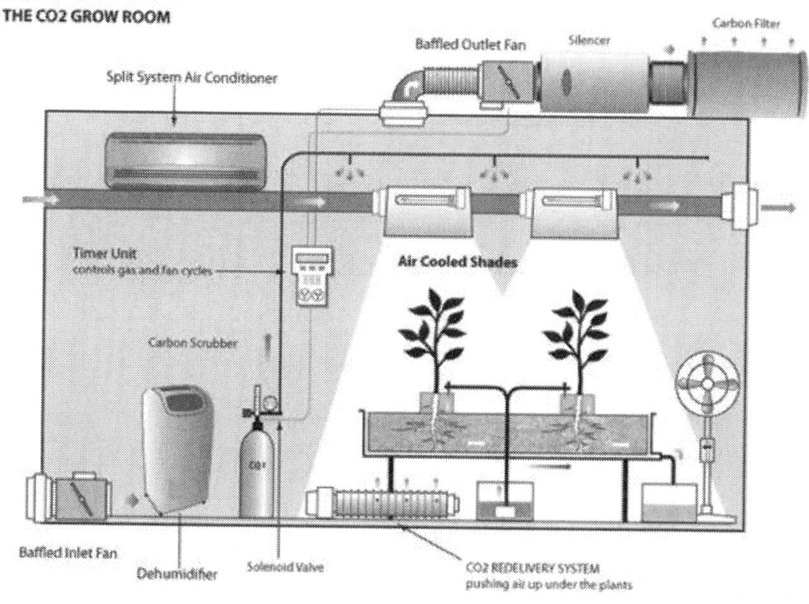

5.10 Water Quality in Hydroponic: PH, EC, and Temperature

Control, increase and decrease of the water values in the Hydroponic system

Hydroponic irrigation of plants is vital because through irrigation - in addition to providing water - all the nutrients the plant needs are also administered.

In hydroponics, water is a much more relevant and vital factor than land cultivation. We must pay close attention to two fundamental parameters the pH and the electrical conductivity, also called EC.

The control of pH in Hydroponics: reference values

The hydroponic pH must be around 5.8 - 6.0. Through a pH meter, we can determine if the solution is acidic or basic.

The optimal pH in hydroponics must be around 5.8 - 6.0.

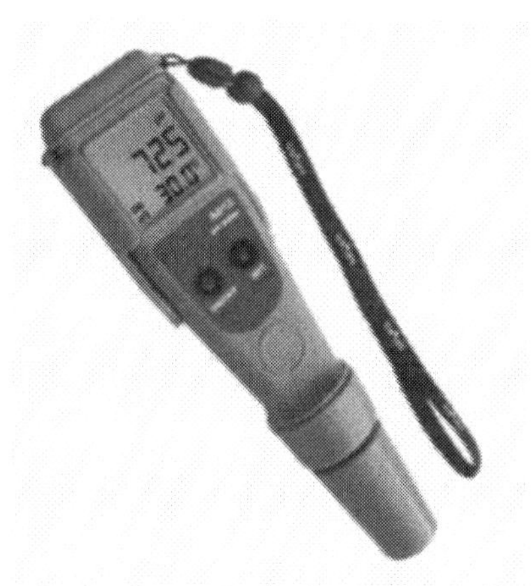

What to do if the pH is too high or too low?

If the solution is too acidic, it will be sufficient to correct it by increasing the pH (pH +), if the water is too basic, we will fix it by decreasing the pH (pH-).

pH- Contains 30% phosphoric acid to reduce the pH value of the nutrient solution.

pH + Contains potassium carbonate to increase the PH value during the growth and flowering phase.

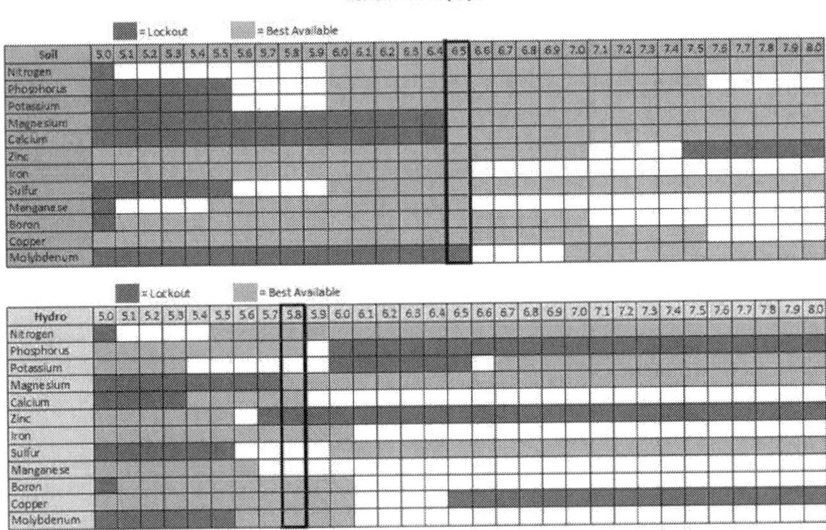

Electrical conductivity control - EC

Electrical or EC conductivity is measured in mS/sec milli-Siemens per second through a conductivity meter. Measuring the EC is used to establish the quantity of salts dissolved in the water.

The salts naturally present in the water of the water network can vary from area to area so often if we are in areas with a high concentration of salts it is preferable to use osmotic water or water that has been previously filtered through a reverse osmosis system that leads to values of water conductivity close to zero.

The recommended electrical conductivity - EC values vary according to the germination and growth / flowering phase

In the germination phase, the Ec must be between a minimum of 0.6 and a maximum of 1.0.

In the growth and flowering phases, the Ec must be between a minimum of 1.0 and a maximum of 2.0.

In the last flowering phase, it is advisable to drop again between a minimum of 0.6 and a maximum of 1.0.

How to adjust the water EC: what to do if the electrical conductivity EC is too high or too low?

When the EC is too low, it is sufficient to increase the amount of fertilizer, while if it is too high, we must decrease the fertilizer.

The water temperature: reference values

The water temperature is critical in hydroponics. In hydroponics, the temperature must be between a minimum of 59°F (15°C) and a maximum of 73°F (23°C).

What to do if the water temperature is too high or too low?

When you introduce new water into the system, pay attention to the starting temperature, and if it is too cold, it is essential to wait until it warms up to room temperature. When the water temperature is too low in production, the ambient temperature is probably also too low. And the same principle applies in the case of too high temperatures. Therefore, before proceeding to raise or lower the water temperature directly, act, and adjust the temperature of the external environment.

5.11 Fertilization of Hydroponics

Fertilizers and nutrients are for plants like food for humans

Fertilizers and nutrients are for plants such as food for humans and are, therefore, a fundamental element in indoor cultivation. There are many types on the market with different characteristics. Still, it is crucial to make sure the fertilizer used is suitable for the kind of cultivation we are carrying out. For example, if we grow in hydroponics, we must use a specific fertilizer for hydroponic cultivation, which will be composed of specific elements suitable on inert substrates such as clay or rock wool.

All fertilizer manufacturers supply the so-called fertigation schemes which are used to synthesize the products and quantities to be administered in the weeks of the plant life cycle. It is advisable to refer to the manufacturer's indications for times and doses of administration.

Organic and Mineral Fertilizers: which to choose and why

Fertilizers provide plants with all the macroelements (Nitrogen, Phosphorus, Potassium) and microelements they need to grow properly and healthily.

Both organic and mineral fertilizers provide plants with the main macroelements for their development. So what are the main differences between the two types of fertilizers?

Organic or Mineral: the release method

The main difference between mineral and organic fertilizers lies in how the elements are released and how they are absorbed by the plants through the soil.

Organic fertilizers - among which we can include guano, manure, dried blood, and bone meal - slowly degrade and are assimilated by plants within weeks or months, unlike mineral ones that break up immediately, and they are readily assimilable.

Which to choose?

Organic fertilizers are indeed indicated for the preparation of the seedbed and for an annual and more natural fertilization (they do not contain chemical impurities). In contrast, mineral fertilizers can be used in the vegetative and productive phase of plants. It is important to underline how the two types of fertilizers are not mutually exclusive, but instead can be used in a complementary way.

But beware of excess fertilization

Whether they are organic or mineral, excess fertilization must always be avoided: an excessive dose can, in fact, irreparably damage the plant and its healthy growth. It is therefore recommended always to respect the doses indicated in the bottle, and in case of excess fertilization, rinse the earth promptly with plenty of water at room temperature.

Chapter 6

BEST PLANTS FOR HYDROPONICS

Plants suitable for Hydroculture

First of all, it is necessary to know that cuttings rooted in water are ideal for starting hydroculture because, for them, it is much easier to adapt to the expanded clay substrate since it is mainly composed of water.

If you want to start with the cultivation of hydroculture plants, there is a great variety to choose from. If you are a lover of aromatic herbs, the rosemary plant is perfect for growing in hydroculture if you start from cutting; otherwise, you can choose other types of ornamental and very decorative plants, such as Ficus, Calathea, Pothos, Dracena, and Philodendron.

All plants characterized by leaves of tropical origin are well suited to hydroculture, such as the orchid and all those species that present a rapid development to the root system.

And what about flowering plants? In these cases, the most recommended species for home hydroculture are Hibiscus, Spathiphyllum, Kalanchoe, Anthurium, or Saintpaulia. Still, nothing prevents you from trying to cultivate other types of plants as well.

What about succulents? Succulents have a more complicated situation since they do not tolerate excess humidity. Therefore the recommended species for hydroculture are aloe, succulent plants, and - as anticipated above - orchids.

6.1 Lettuce

Growing salad in hydroponics is elementary, much more than it might seem, even for those who start from scratch and approach the hydroponics world for the first time.

Once you have identified the variety of salad that best suits your needs and tastes, you must obtain the seeds that you will easily find online. Then you will have to buy rock wool cubes (Rockwool) and net jars, a mini-green to store them in the warm, in a protected environment and with net pots, designed precisely for the needs of plants that are grown with hydroponic and aeroponic systems. Therefore, a small hydroponic or aeroponic system will be needed.

The salad seeds must be placed inside the moistened rock wool cubes (it is recommended not to insert more than five seeds for each cube) only with water and then placed inside the mini-greenhouse, at a temperature that can oscillate between 73°F (23°C) and 82°F (28°C).

One aspect to check - when using rock wool cubes - is the amount of water they absorb, because an excessive amount of liquid could cause the roots to rot and drown them. For this, it is always advisable to check the liquid levels present and possibly wring out the cubes to let out the excess water.

With the right amount of water and the ideal temperature, lettuce seeds will begin to germinate after about 48 hours. When you see the first roots appearing from the rock wool cubes (both from the sides and the base), it means that the time has come to transfer the newly born seedlings to the special mesh pots, which will first be filled with expanded clay and then settled in the hydroponic system you have chosen (or aeroponic). The seedlings inserted in the aeroponic system will then be fed with a special nutrient solution based on water and fertilizers to provide everything they need. It is vital to avoid any fertilizer during the germination phase and then start with a halved dose compared to what is recommended on the package.

Fertilizers for the cultivation of Hydroponic salad

By using suitable fertilizers and in the right dose, the roots of the lettuce seedlings are allowed to develop better and faster than they would use with a traditional cultivation system, also because - in this way - the roots can receive and assimilate nutrients faster.

To grow the seedlings in a healthy and fast way, thus strengthening their root system to make it more robust, it is possible to opt for some special fertilizers, which contain fundamental substances capable of promoting and increasing growth, accelerating absorption nutrients, and keep the most common salad diseases away. Fertilizers play a central role in the life and health of the plant. Since the hydroponic and aeroponic system does not provide for the presence of fertile soil, to ensure that the salad receives all the nutrients, it is essential to use the right fertilizers to be able to grow plants properly. Strengthening the root system of salad plants and preventing pests means growing healthy, strong, and vigorous plants capable of returning a good harvest.

Hydroponic salad: parameters to monitor

At this point, once the cultivation has started, it is appropriate to keep under control some fundamental values for the health and growth of each plant, such as the pH, which will determine the ability - by the cultivated plant - to correctly absorb the available nutrients.

In order for salad plants to absorb all nutrients correctly, the pH must be slightly acidic, and to ensure that it is always such, it is advisable to often monitor the situation with manual tests. For example, cheap and easy-to-use paper strips for pH testing can be used.

Tips and tricks for a perfect Hydroponic salad

To create a suitable and protected environment, it is recommended to repair and check the salad plants inside a grow box to make them grow well, healthily and faster, without weighing on the cost of the bill.

Among the advantages of using the grow box, there is undoubtedly that of being able to more easily control the temperature than a larger environment and, therefore, less controlled, better manage ventilation, ensure the right lighting (thanks to the reflective mylar sheet present inside the grow box which allows the light to be effectively propagated).

But when will you get your first salad crop?

Much depends on the variety chosen and cultivated, but - in general - it is possible to say that the time required varies between 4 weeks and 80 days. By choosing different varieties and managing the aeroponic system, you can have a fresh, tasty, and healthy salad at any time of the year.

To help grow, salad plants should be adequately lit: the best solution is to use HID discharge lamps or LEDs, but a good compromise can also be found by using fluorescent lamps.

To better manage the lighting of the salad plants, it is advisable to activate the lights for 12 hours a day, thus ensuring 12 hours of darkness.

For beginners, it is advisable to purchase a simple lighting set consisting of 4 CFL lamps, sufficient for home cultivation.

6.2 Strawberries

Cross and delight of many professional and amateur growers, the strawberry is a problematic fruit, especially if grown out of season and in unsuitable environments. All difficulties are overcome, especially for those who choose the above-ground cultivation, better known as hydroponic cultivation.

The more than tested technique, especially in strawberry cultivation, offers more than exciting advantages:

- production is standardized;

- there is a considerable saving of energy and water, which is used more rationally;

- production is better in quality and quantity;

- the problem of diseases, molds, and pests that multiply on contact with the ground are entirely forgotten.

Those who choose the hydroponic technique also have the opportunity to produce strawberries in at least two different periods of the year: from October to December and throughout April and May.

If we also take into consideration that once planted, the plants begin to bear fruit after 45 days. It is well understood why this choice is shared by many growers and lovers of indoor cultivation.

Anyone who chooses to switch to this type of technique must first thoroughly wash the roots of their seedlings and insert them in a small pot that contains expanded clay or alchemy of vermiculite and perlite.

It is also essential to have a container that can hold at least 10 liters of water (for each seedling), better if impermeable to the passage of light to avoid the formation of algae and mushrooms.

Among the most popular hydroponic cultivation methods for strawberries, there is the one called NFT hydroponics: to make it simple with this system; it is possible to achieve a good circulation of all the nutrients that the roots need. Everything is automated thanks to the use of a timer that alternates between full and dry moments, essential for the roots to have the right oxygenation.

Obviously, it is essential to have the right fertilizer, which in this case, is composed of nitrogen and potassium and water with the correct pH, which should always be adjusted between 5.5 and 5.6. To make the job easier, there are active acidity regulators on the market.

Finally, you must have the right lighting, and in this case, the lamps for indoor cultivation will be a potent ally.

Once you start your strawberry cultivation, domestic or industrial, it is good to keep in mind that the plant must be regularly pruned: it is wrong not to cut excess leaves, especially before flowering. These will unnecessarily weaken the plant and could favor the creation of mushrooms that are particularly harmful to the future growth of strawberries.

Also, despite the impatience shared by many growers, it is good that the fruit is harvested only when red and ripe, better still if in times of darkness.

6.3 Tomatoes

Quality and quantity with Hydroponic tomato cultivation

Tomato is a genuinely functional vegetable in hydroponic culture. It reacts very well to the so-called "soilless cultivation," this because it can easily adapt to different types of substrate and does not require demanding agronomic management.

In tomato hydroponics, multiple substrates can be used:

- Rock wool
- Peat
- Perlite
- Coconut fiber
- Compost

And with all, you can achieve magnificent results. The only precaution that must be paid in the hydroponic cultivation of tomatoes is the temperature. Indeed, excessive maxims could affect the floral drop and, therefore, on the quantity and quality of the product.

6.4 Kitchen herbs

The new home dream is to have a thousand and one aromatic herbs on the terrace or the balcony to flavor your dishes with a personal, fresh, and eco-friendly touch. This is why hydroponics has been so successful.

The Greeks already knew it, Francis Bacon spoke about it in 1627 and today hydroponics (literally the art of growing plants in water) is well appreciated in the industrial and domestic field.

The hydroponic cultivation of aromatic herbs has five remarkable qualities:

1. the yield of the product that is developed through indoor cultivation is better;

2. growth is faster;

3. the taste is more intense;

4. the cultivation technique is environmentally sustainable;

5. the water expenditure decreases drastically.

With hydroponic cultivation at home, it is possible to grow any aromatic plant, whether it is parsley, basil, thyme, rosemary, oregano. Still, you can also choose to grow lettuces, tomatoes, strawberries, and who knows what else.

In short, hydroponics allows at reduced costs and with a disarming simplicity to make your terrace or balcony a garden of wonders, a vertical garden, an urban oasis.

The roots of our aromatic seedlings will seek support on an inert substrate often made up of expanded clay, pralines, coconut fiber, or other similar materials. Of course, the irrigation that the plant receives must be rich in inorganic compounds that will be able to give it all the nutrients that generally come from the earth. Your cultivation of aromatic herbs will surely provide unparalleled satisfaction.

6.5 Orchids

Orchids lend themselves perfectly to hydroculture. They are, in fact, epiphytic plants (i.e., plants that naturally grow and live on other plants), and humid environments represent their ideal condition for growing well and in health. The plant will develop its roots, which - with the growth and passage of time - will pass through the holes of the pot, to flow directly into the water. Different varieties of orchids can be grown in hydroculture, such as the best-known variety of Phalaenopsis, but also Cattleya, the Dendrobium variety, Paphiopedilum and Oncidium.

One of the main advantages offered by this cultivation technique is represented by the opportunity to supply the plant with a constant quantity of water capable of properly hydrating and irrigating the orchid without damaging it with an excess of liquid. All this - combined with correct fertilization - allows the plant to grow at a much faster rate than traditional cultivation techniques.

Another advantage of orchids grown in hydroculture is given by the typical characteristics of expanded clay, used in these cases instead of the soil or the mix of materials generally used for orchids, which allows faster, easier, and risk-free repotting to damage the roots.

In this way, orchids quickly develop their root system: in a short time, the roots will grow and pass through the holes of the pot in which they are located and will begin to develop directly in the cultivation water.

By doing so, orchid plants will grow faster and healthier, without any disadvantages.

As already mentioned, there are many benefits of using the hydroculture method:

The plant needs much less maintenance

Faster and faster growth

A reduction in the risk of pests and diseases

Greater oxygenation of the roots

Elimination of mold and other allergens.

6.6 Plants to avoid in Hydroponic cultivation

Some plants are not precisely indicated in hydroponic cultivation. Here are a few:

Pumpkins

Pumpkins love the sun and well-drained soil with neutral pH.

They are challenging to grow in a hydroponic system as they have large groups of roots that spread rapidly.

Squash

Squash grows at the base of the plant, which means it could rest on damp soils. This will likely encourage mushroom growth.

Also, squash is generally a large plant with minimal yield. There are much better ways to use space in the hydroponic system.

Zucchini

This is a great plant, which means it will need a lot of support. It needs more nutrients than other plants and won't give such a significant yield for space.

It is necessary to keep the temperature around 75 ° F (24 ° C), even during the night. It will also dry out very quickly if it does not have enough water and nutrients.

Potatoes

Most root vegetables are not suitable for hydroponic systems. Potatoes are such a case.

The cost of the harvest will be very low compared to the efforts needed to grow it.

Radish

Some plants will grow well, but they are still not a good option. You need the right supports to make them grow hydroponically, and in the end, the cost will probably be higher than buying in a store.

Chapter 7

HYDROPONICS VS AQUAPONICS

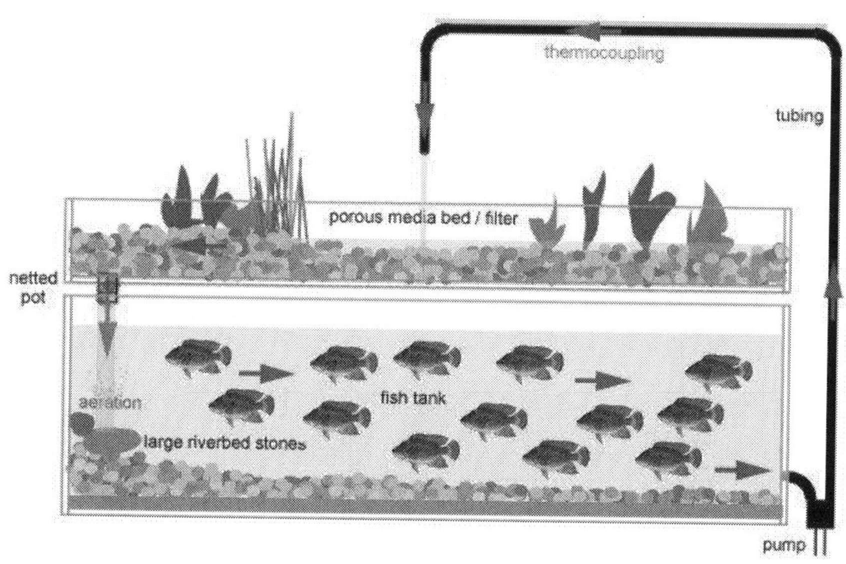

With an aquaponics system, it is possible to use 1/10 of the amount of water generally used for the irrigation of traditional crops in soil: even less water than the quantities used in hydroponic cultivation. Furthermore, being a natural ecosystem, it is not possible to use harmful petrochemical products, pesticides, or herbicides.

To feed it and make it work, feed the fish in the system and collect the plants that will develop.

Among the advantages offered by this type of system, there is undoubtedly great freedom in choosing the place; in fact, it is possible to grow anywhere: at home or in a garage, in a greenhouse, or in a courtyard to be set up as you prefer. But there is more because everything is scalable: based on the available budget, it is possible to choose the size and space to be dedicated to this type of system, which can be expanded even later.

In fact, aquaponics offers the possibility of growing anywhere, even vertically, and thus producing a large quantity of food in minimal space. In tower aquaponic systems - for example - the plants are stacked on each other, the water comes down from the top of the tower and reaches the roots and then falls directly into the fish tank.

Among the ideal cultivation systems for aquaponics, there is undoubtedly the DWC (deep water culture), which provides a large cultivation container, low and wide, which floats in a channel full of water from fish and appropriately filtered to remove the solid waste. The plants are placed in special holes created within the cultivation plan; here, the roots of the plants are free and in contact with the underlying water. This method is ideal for growing salads and other vegetables that grow rapidly and don't need large quantities of nutrients.

Another system widely used in aquaponic cultivation is the TFT (Nutrient film Technique), which provides for the presence of a slightly inclined tank on the bottom of which a mat rich in nutrients is applied.

Inside the tank, water flows, which takes the nutrients from the film placed on the bottom and distributes them to the roots of the plants that directly touch the water flow.

The plants are arranged inside holes made in a tube placed above the inclined tank: in this way, the roots hang freely in this continuous flow of water. This cultivation method works very well for plants that need little support, such as strawberries and broad-leaved vegetables, for example.

The NFT system is also a great way to develop crops vertically and use unused space because it can be hung from the ceiling above other crops.

How does Aquaponics work?

Aquaponics effectively transforms the cultivation plant into a small, completely autonomous ecosystem, in which water is continuously recovered, and waste is recycled from the roots.

The combination of water, fish, and plants represents the ideal opportunity to discover, deepen, and convey the importance of self-sufficiency and sustainability. The aquaponic cultivation system is characterized by a recirculation system, where the water - with the help of suitable pumps - is taken from the tank where the fish are located and conveyed into a filter, which carries out the nitrification process, bringing the formation of nitrite and nitrate destined to be assimilated by plants.

In essence, the water collects and transports all the liquid. Solid waste naturally produced by fish (which without polluting it pollutes the environment), and the system filters them thanks to the help of beneficial bacteria, which transform them into nutrients. At this point, the now purified nutrient solution returns to the plants' disposal, to guarantee them the right nutrients, and then is put back into the fish breeding tank, thus closing the cycle. In this way, the waste is eliminated, and the plants get the right amount of nutrients without the need for additional nutrients.

Which plants can be grown with Aquaponics?

The varieties of plants that can be grown with the aquaponics method are many, potentially all; in particular, all those that do not need specialized supports to grow, including broad-leaved vegetables, salads, courgettes, aubergines, and aromatic herbs.

What fish for Aquaponics?

As for the fish that can be used within an aquaculture system, it is possible to choose any freshwater fish, including prawns. Of course, depending on the type of fish chosen, it is necessary to set the system differently, based on the characteristics of the variety selected, in order to ensure the right amount and type of nutrients for the plants.

What do you need to create an Aquaculture facility?

To build an aquaculture plant from scratch, it is necessary to purchase a tank intended for breeding fish, a hydroponic tank equipped with a pump - which will be positioned above that of the fish - in which plants will be placed, bacteria that allow the decomposition of the waste of the fish, filters, a kit to measure and adjust the pH, supplements to solve any problems and nutritional deficiencies and then, of course, the fish you prefer and the plants to grow.

To start aquaculture with serenity, it is advisable to purchase a system and ready-to-use kits, which will only need to be assembled and set up following the instructions on the package.

In general, the start-up and maintenance of an aquaponic system does not require great care and attention, but - like all crops of this type, including hydroponics and aeroponics - it requires some checks, such as adequate temperature, pH, humidity (here the section dedicated to conductivity meters), correct ventilation and aeration, (here the section dedicated to air extractors), surface cleaning and the right amount of nutrients (therefore correct number of fish).

One of the crucial aspects to consider at the beginning, in fact, is precisely the relationship - which must be well balanced - between the number and type of plants chosen and the number and breed of fish you wish to breed.

In this way, you can guarantee a healthy and efficient environment.

The other factor to always keep in mind is the nourishment provided to the fish, which must be highly qualitative and supplied in the right doses in order to guarantee the balance of the environment.

Chapter 8

HYDROPONICS VS AEROPONICS

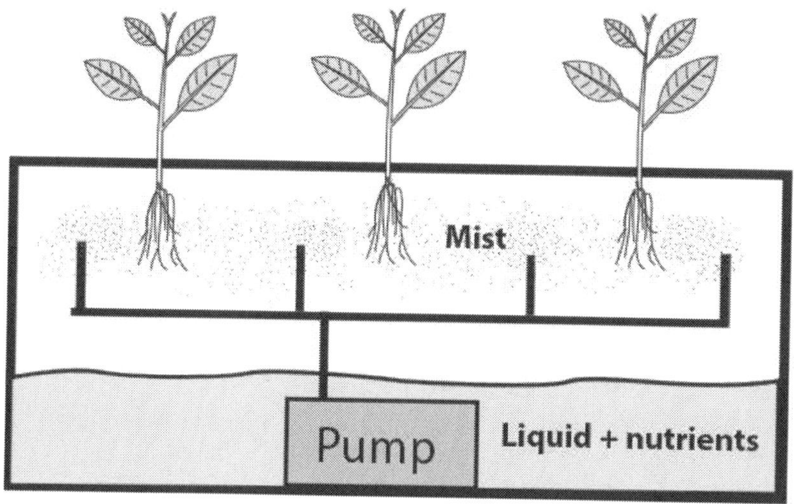

In hydroponic cultivation, as mentioned several times, plants are grown in the absence of land and with the use of water. In general, it is possible to say that with this technique, plants grow thanks to the action of water enriched with nutrients. In a first period, the plants are started inside inert substrates, such as coconut fiber, perlite, expanded clay, or other materials useful for the realization of substrates, to then pass into hydroponic systems, which provide, in addition to correct water supply, thanks to the presence of ad hoc lamps, the temperature, humidity and the right ventilation of the environment.

Aeroponics is an alternative form of growing plants, vegetables, and fruits that do not require the use of land or water.

With this cultivation technique, plants live and grow brilliantly and healthy thanks to the nebulization of a nutrient solution, based on water and substances useful for growth, which is delivered to the roots with a special spray.

This technique should not be confused with hydroponics, where the most crucial element is not air, as in this case, but water.

Once the aeroponic system is set up, the plants are suspended with the roots in the air inside a grow room (or cultivation chamber) where they will remain until the moment of collection.

The basis of growth and plant health is undoubtedly the constant control of temperature, humidity, and lighting.

Pros and Cons of Hydroponics

We have already said several times that the advantages of using a hydroponic system certainly concern reduced maintenance, the possibility of cultivating at any time of the year, and the opportunity to control the climate of the cultivation environment.

More generally, the great advantage of hydroponics is in complete control over nutrients and, therefore, on the growth of plants. Furthermore, hydroponically grown plants perform better than plants grown in the soil. Many systems of this type recycle water and reduce waste.

These soil-free cultivation systems use only 10% of the amount of water needed for conventional crops and are fairly easy to build and assemble. Hydroponic gardens do not require the use of herbicides or pesticides, precisely because weeds do not grow there, they need little space and do not depend on the growing seasons, because they use lamplight, which can be installed anywhere.

However, hydroponic gardens have some cons; for example, if the temperature is too high or too low, even for a single day, the plants could die or otherwise suffer severe damage. Also, the purchase of hydroponic systems and accessories may require a significant expense, especially if you are not an expert.

Pros and Cons of Aeroponics

Among the advantages of aeroponics, there is, in the absolute first place, the efficiency and cleanliness of the cultivation environment.

With this technique, excellent and thriving crops are obtained in a short period. Another significant advantage is the slight risk of contracting bacterial diseases and infections. On the other hand, a disadvantage, especially if you are a beginner, lies in the rather high cost, because it requires the purchase of a series of equipment. Also, it is necessary to have a dedicated indoor room, where you can install the aeroponic system.

Hydroponics and Aeroponics: similarities and differences

The hydroponic and aeroponic systems have many points in common: aeroponics is, in reality, a particular type of hydroponic culture, which also uses the benefits of air. To simplify and summarize, we can say that aeroponics is an evolution of hydroponics, to get the most out of the potential of plants in terms of yield and speed.

The main difference between the two techniques is that hydroponic systems come in many forms: plants can be suspended in water full time, or a continuous or intermittent flow can feed them. In a hydroponic system, plants grow with water and without soil, with the help of inert substrates. The two systems have in common the supply of nutrients that are delivered directly from the source and supplied to the roots.

The plants in aeroponics, however, are never placed in the water but sprayed at a distance thanks to a dispenser that hydrates and nourishes the roots several times an hour, thanks to an automated system that guarantees regularity and punctuality. One reason these two cultivation methods have so much in common is that aeroponics is, in reality, a type of hydroponics. The main difference is that hydroponic systems can be of various types: there are different types, and for this, you can choose the one that best suits your needs.

A disadvantage common to both hydroponic and aeroponic cultivation systems is that relying on automated systems that require, therefore, electricity, they could require the use of expensive generators to be used in case of power outages. However, once set up and started, hydroponic and aeroponic systems allow you to save significantly compared to traditional cultivation techniques.

According to current phenomena, it is possible that forms of hydroponic and aeroponic agriculture will increase in popularity over time and become commonplace in all of our homes. What is certain is that due to climate change and the unregulated action of man, the quantity of soil available for cultivation will tend to decrease, and its quality will continue to deteriorate. Therefore more and more people will try to produce healthy food in their homes (many have already started to grow salads, tomatoes, strawberries, etc.). Hydroponic and aeroponic gardens and orchards can provide the right answer to these growing needs.

Chapter 9

IT'S TIME TO TRY!

Building a hydroponic system is a great adventure.

At first, everything may seem complicated, and there is a lot of information to assimilate, but now you have the basis for doing it.

Research, study, design, and modify according to your needs.

With the hydroponic system, cultures grow very fast, allowing you to test, experiment, do, and modify quickly.

And once you find yourself in a thousand shades of green, you will surely be rewarded for every effort made.

HYDROPONICS

21 LITTLE-KNOWN SECRETS TO BUILD YOUR HYDROPONIC GARDEN

James Water

Chapter 1

HYDROPONIC CULTIVATION

Hydroponics, or more correctly and in a general sense, soilless cultivation is a technology aimed at growing plants in a nutrient solution (water that contains nutrients) with or without the use of an artificial medium (sand, gravel, vermiculite, perlite, rock wool, etc.).

Liquid hydroponic systems have no other means of supporting the roots of plants; systems in a solid medium, instead, use a substrate as support.

Soil-free cultivation systems are also classified as open (when the nutrient solution draining from the roots is not reused) or closed (when the surplus solution is collected, corrected, and returned to the system).

Soil-free crops are mostly grown in the greenhouse, often requiring high technology and substantial capital. However, they are very productive, ergonomic, efficiently use space water, and (potentially) protect the environment.

Since in such agricultural systems the regulation of the air and radical environment is one of the main aspects, the production takes place through the parallel control of the temperatures of the air and of the roots, of the light, of the relative humidity of the air, of the water, plant nutrition and climatic adversities.

We will see below 21 little-known secrets that will help you to build your hydroponic garden.

Chapter 2

THE ADVANTAGES AND DISADVANTAGES OF HYDROPONIC CULTURES

Before starting a DIY hydroculture system, it would be good to be aware of what you are going through.

There are, in fact, numerous pros and cons in starting any production system.

We will now see some advantages together.

It is possible to grow hydroponically anywhere in the world

The only necessary condition is to have water available!

There are many geographical areas in the world, such as deserts or dry regions, where nothing can be cultivated in the soil. Here, if we can have water, we can grow with a hydroponic system.

Keep pests under control

Soil is not present in the hydroponic system, and this means reducing the risk of disease because plants are often attacked by soil-borne pests.

It is, however, important to specify that the problem of parasites is not totally eliminated because our plants can be attacked by air parasites and have diseases.

Greenhouses or indoor growing setups act as a barrier for pests.

We can use beneficial insects that eat pests that we will release in our greenhouses or hydroponic systems.

We will deal extensively with this topic.

Take less time to grow your vegetables

Compared to traditional culture methods, hydroponics provides better results.

The plants are supplied with all the necessary nutrients and trace elements; they will, therefore, grow faster and be more resistant to pests.

Keep everything under control

By growing in hydroponics, you can keep under control, monitor, and regulate all the nutrients that are supplied to plants.

It is, therefore, possible to improve the performance of your production over time.

Use less water and don't waste it

Compared to plants that are grown in the traditional field, many types of research have shown that hydroponics needs about 90% less water.

With this type of cultivation, we lose water only by evaporation or various exchanges, most of which are put back into circulation in the system.

As always, however, we must also take into account some disadvantages:

Rather high setup costs

Several elements are needed to start and install a hydroponic system. This obviously entails higher start-up costs compared to soil crops.

You will need:

- a water tank
- a pump for water re-circulation
- a setup for plant growth
- a growing substrate
- nutrients and fertilizers
- artificial lights.

Possibility of contracting airborne diseases

We have already said that the chance of contracting diseases that can be transmitted to the soil is considerably less; despite this, there are diseases that are carried in the air and can affect the plants that we grow in hydroponics. Since these plants are very close to each other, we pay attention because they could spread quickly.

If we know the initial and primary signs of the diseases, we can intervene quickly and eradicate them.

The Pythium (root rot), instead, spreads through the water. The consequence will be the brow of the roots. We design the system correctly, and we will be able to keep everything under control.

It is necessary to know

To make the whole system work properly, it is essential to understand how the various necessary equipment works and to be able to monitor nutrient levels.

Understanding the principles of hydroponic culture is quite simple, but, as with all that is unknown, we must read, study, and learn.

Electricity is essential

Your electricity bill will suffer from a higher cost as power is needed to operate the pumps, heat, cold, and circulate the air and use artificial lights.

You also need to pay close attention to your safety as water and electricity don't work well together.

Plants could suffer a lot if something happens to the electrical system or the power supply is interrupted. It would be advantageous to have a generator or solar system to run the system for a few hours.

It is necessary to monitor

Growing in hydroponic, unlike in the soil where we can afford to ignore our plants for a few days, and they will survive, presupposes the control and surveillance of everything.

A mechanical or electrical failure will kill our seedlings or otherwise have a disastrous effect.

But don't worry, there are many ways to automate every part of the system and make things easier for us. And so you can easily dedicate yourself to your favorite hobby.

Chapter 3

21 LITTLE-KNOWN SECRETS TO BUILD YOUR HYDROPONIC GARDEN

1. The essential accessories for each grower

When preparing the grow room for indoor growing, you could think of all those great things you will need: substrate, tent, lights, air extraction, nutrients, and seeds. These are the most obvious things to think about, but they are the smallest (even the most important!) Things that are often forgotten. So with this concept in mind, we have compiled a list of essential accessories that will improve your grow room by making it more organized.

Syringes or Pipettes

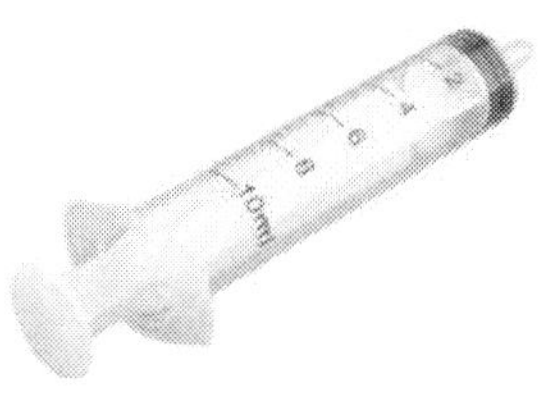

Syringes, graduated pipettes, and measuring spoons are indispensable elements for mixing the right amount of fertilizer and water, adding pH correctors, or for making any dosage of small quantities of liquids.

Scissors

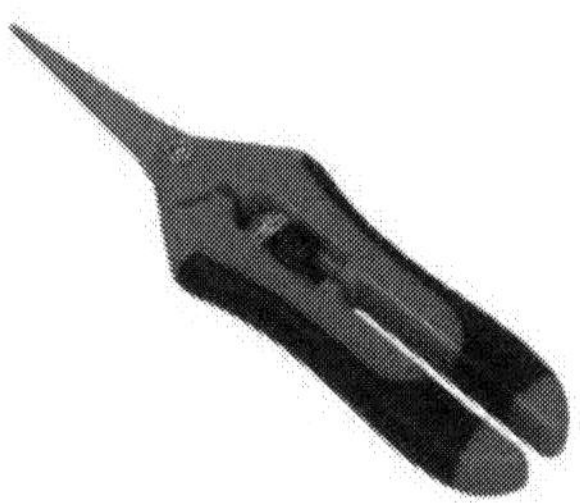

The scissors are the faithful ally of the indoor grower, only if they are well cleaned and sharp. It is vital to keep the scissors clean to avoid transmitting bacteria to plants.

Thermo-hygrometer

Hygrometer thermometers, also commonly called Thermo hygrometers, are indispensable tools for monitoring and measuring temperatures and humidity in the grow room. It is essential in the cultivation area to have a real-time reading of the climatic status of the cultivation area, and in the case to intervene in time to correct too low or high temperature and humidity

Timer for lights

A timer will keep your daylight cycle running smoothly. It will allow you to precisely program the switching on and off of the indoor lights without having to do it manually. In short, a faithful ally. We advise you not to use cheap, inexpensive timers, as they do not work with large current flows and can, in the worst case, cause a fire, the last thing you need in your grow room!

pH meter

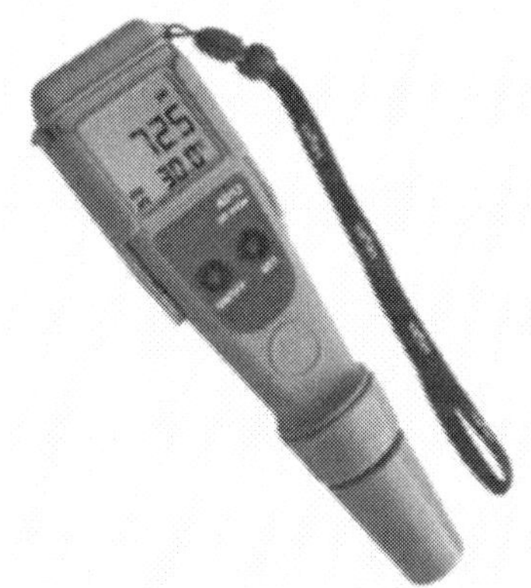

Measuring the pH of the nutrient solution is essential for keeping plants healthy. Periodic verification of the nutrient solution with a pH meter allows your plants to get what they need.

Hangers

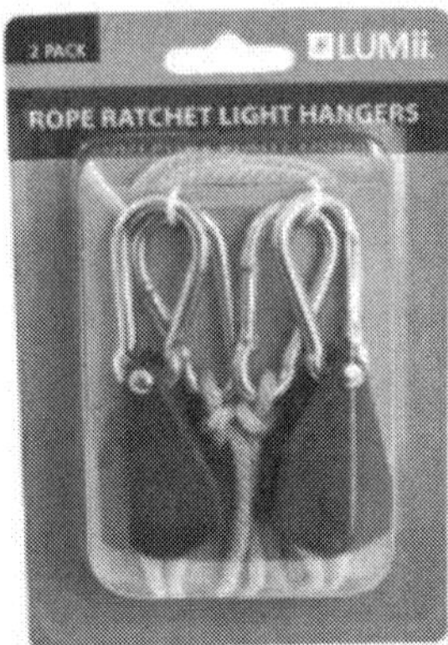

The pulleys allow hanging the reflector of the lighting system on the grow box. With the hangers, it is possible to position the reflector at the desired distance from the plants, making it rise and fall effortlessly.

Labels for plants

The most apparent use for labels is to identify the type of plant, strain, or selection that is grown. But that's not all as they can be used to indicate other information regarding the plant, such as the fertilization regime, the number of growth or flowering weeks, signs of deficiencies, and any other specifics of the plant.

Cloth tape

If there is a product with which you cannot live without, it is the adhesive tape. In indoor cultivation, as at home, it can be handy for repairing small things and for completely isolating connections. For example, it can be used to connect the air extractor to the aluminum duct or to repair small tears in cultivation tents. These are just some of the useful uses of cloth tape.

Power strip - extension

Sometimes a socket is not enough to connect all the accessories of indoor cultivation, therefore resorting to a power strip is a convenient solution. You can connect the lights timer, the air extractor, and a possible clip fan in a single socket. A high-quality power strip guarantees the safety of the connected electrical appliances. It is crucial to choose a good extension with the correct wattage/amperage to avoid short and, in the worst-case fires.

Head torch

The headlamp with the green color spectrum allows you to have your hands free while inspecting the plants during the dark period, without altering the photo-period. Some operations are to be carried out during the dark hours in indoor cultivation, such as the application of a foliar spray. The lights intensity can cause burns on the leaves and flowers, and thus ruin the health of the plant.

Plant tie rod

It can happen, especially during the growth phase, a disordered jungle is formed. Having available wires or tie rods allows you to arrange the plants without damaging them to allow all the leaves to receive the right amount of light.

2. DIY Hydroculture with germinated plants

To start with the cultivation of plants in hydroculture, you must first extract the plant from its pot and gently remove all the soil that surrounds the roots. At this point, dip the roots in warm water to cleanse them: at this point, the plant can be transferred inside a special pot.

The pots used for hydroculture are two and are placed one inside the other. The plant and the expanded clay are inserted inside the smaller pot, which will serve to keep the vegetable in a straight position; this jar will then be inserted into a second larger jar, which contains the water and the nutrient solution.

The water level indicator is fundamental for growing plants with hydroculture: an instrument placed inside the pot, which helps to remember and signal when you need to add more water, or when the liquid level will have gone down to the minimum.

At this point, it will be essential to prepare the smallest container, which consists of a transparent plastic full of holes on the surface: insert a layer of expanded clay of about two centimeters. Once this is done, it will be necessary to arrange the plant and then gently cover it with other clay to guarantee its stability.

Once the plant has been arranged, it will be necessary to prepare the largest pot, the external one, characterized by walls without holes. This container must also be filled with expanded clay, just like the space between the two pots, remembering to also insert, in the special compartment, the water level indicator.

Finally, water will be added to the largest and most external container until it reaches the maximum height on the indicator.

3. How to start with seeds

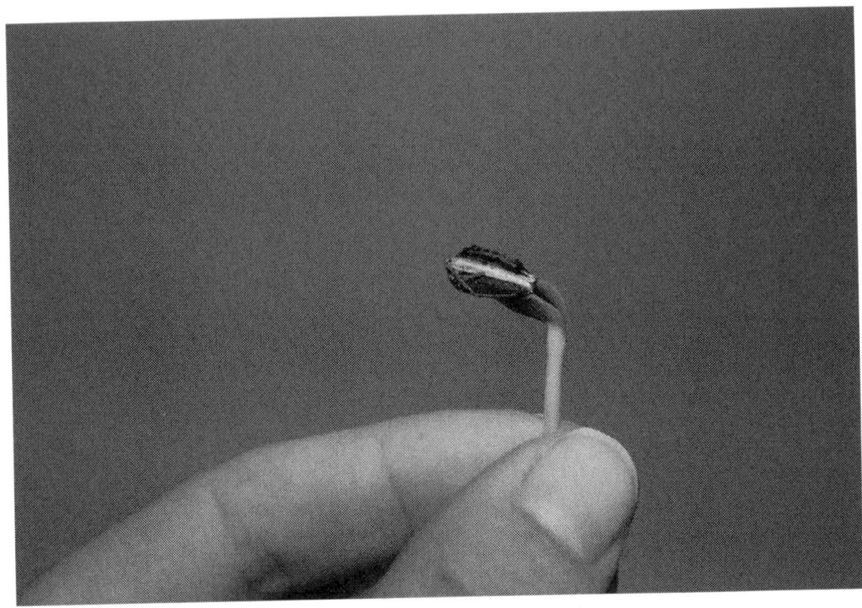

It is most satisfying plant a seed and nurture it until it becomes a full-grown plant and provides with the intended harvest. Of course, it takes more effort to grow a plant from seed than it does from a seedling. It is good to decide if this is the preferred method and discover the best way of starting seeds. Hydroponics is an excellent system for starting seeds as we have complete control over the elements your seeds are exposed to.

Seeds or Seedlings

For the first attempt at hydroponics, it is quicker to plant seedlings. However, controlling all the elements of the growing process includes monitoring the seeds. If you decide to plant seeds, you will have complete control over the type and quality of the seed you plant.

Put simply; you can have any variety of seed but not necessarily any variety of seedling. Seeds are generally easier to get hold of then seedlings.

The other consideration is the growing media. In hydroponics, you avoid using soil. However, unless you have a hydroponic center near you, the seedlings you purchase are likely to be grown in soil. You should carefully remove the soil to avoid contamination of your system. Unfortunately, washing them can damage the roots of the seedling.

Besides, seeds are cheaper than seedlings, allowing you more opportunities for failure without breaking the bank.

With proper planning and equipment, you are better off growing the plants from seed.

Starting the seeds

The best way to start seeds is to use a seed starter cube. A cube, the size of one and a half inch will fit perfectly in a two-inch net pot. These small cubes are capable of holding water while air can reach the roots, which is the most important while germinating seeds.

First, you need to soak your grow cubes in chlorine or chloramine free water with a pH of 5.5.

Water from your tap will be around 7-8 pH. You most likely need to use a pH down solution.

Getting the chlorine out of your tap water is quite easy. Let it sit for one day for the chlorine to evaporate. If you want it to evaporate faster, you can use an air stone to air the chlorine out much quicker.

If your water company uses chloramine, you need a reverse osmosis filter to remove the chloramine. Note that not every reverse osmosis filter can remove chloramine. Chloramine can't be aired out and needs to be filtered. If you do not have a reverse osmosis filter available, you can use one thousand mg (one gram) of vitamin C (ascorbic acid) per forty gallons (one hundred and fifty liters) of water.

Use a tray to soak the cubes, pour the water on top, and let it sit for a few minutes. Once most of the water is absorbed, you need to drain the rest of the water. Do not squeeze the cubes. This will remove air pockets inside the cubes.

The next step is dropping your seeds into the holes. This can be a big task if you need to do a lot of seeds. Commercial growers use pelleted seeds and a vacuum seeder to speed this process up. Pelleted seed is a seed that is wrapped in clay. It is bigger, thus more comfortable to handle.

You could also use a toothpick and dip the tip in some water. This will make the seed stick to the toothpick, and it will make it a little easier.

If the holes of the grow media are preventing you from dropping the seed in, use a pen or a toothpick to open the hole back up.

You can use more than one seed per hole if the germination rate is bad. I always use two seeds per hole. When both seeds germinate, keep the best one and use scissors to remove the bad one.

Next, place your humidity dome on top of the tray to keep the seed starter cubes moist. Generally, the seeds don't need water until they have germinated. If you notice that your seed starter cubes are drying out, you can pour some more water in the tray. Don't forget to drain the rest of the water.

Once the seeds start showing its first two leaves, you need to put it under a light source. This will provide the plant with the energy they need to grow. If you experience that the stems are growing long (stretching) It means that your plant is reaching for the light. Increase the light on the seedlings to avoid this stretching. Do not use the red light on seedlings. White fluorescents that are 6500K are perfect.

After ten days, you can transplant them to your system. If you are growing in a greenhouse, it can take fifteen days in winter.

Heat mats will increase germination during colder weather. The mats are placed under the seedling tray to warm up the seed starting cubes. Setting the heat mat to 68°F (20°C) is recommended.

Recap:

1.Soak your seed starting cubes in chlorine or chloramine free water. Distilled water is even better. Make sure the pH is around 5.5.

2.Put the seed starting cubes in a tray.

3.Put the seed in the holes of the seed starter cubes.

4.Cover the seed starting cubes with a humidity dome.

5.Set the heat mat to 68°F (20°C) and place it under the tray.

6.Once sprouts appear, water them from the bottom with one quarter nutrient strength. The cubes will wick up the water.

7.Place them under T5 fluorescent lights. The humidity dome is still on the tray.

8.When you see four leaves and the roots are developing out of the seed starting cubes, it is time to transplant them to your growing system.

Nutrients during seeding.

Seeds don't need nutrients initially as they are self-contained. However, you can give them a quarter-strength solution, compared to what you are using in your adult plant hydroponic system.

4. The best substrate for Hydroponic cultivation of plants

The substrate, or cultivation medium, is the substance where plants are sown and grown.

In hydroponic cultivation, although it is not a real soil, it is the place where the root system of plants will have to expand. The substrate itself does not contain nutrients, and, for this reason, it is called an inert substrate. Due to this specific characteristic, which differentiates it from ordinary soil or cultivation soil, it becomes necessary to water it, continuously or at intervals, with the nutrient solution.

However, it is necessary to know that, for many varieties of plants, the use of a substrate is not essential because it is possible to grow them directly in the nutrient solution.

In hydroponic crops, the general orientation is to use highly efficient substrates that can be recovered, both to be able to use them in multiple cultivation cycles and to be able to recycle them. For example, when they no longer perform their function, they can be inserted and reused in the industry or construction market.

Which substrates are suitable for Hydroponic cultivation?

The best substrates for amateur and professional hydroponic cultivation will be described below:

Rock wool, Rockwool and Grodan slabs

Rock wool is a soft, very porous material and therefore has low water retention despite having, on the other hand, a great ability to circulate a lot of oxygen. This material is not biodegradable and is sold in cubes (Rockwool cubes) or plates (Rockwool slab). It is possible to use rock wool in various hydroponic cultivation techniques, such as sack culture, or active drip hydroponic systems. Often, more in professional hydroponic cultivation, rock wool is used for the germination of seeds in hydroponic seedbeds. It can be sown in slabs or cubes of rock wool as long as it is introduced into a container on the bottom of which one or two centers of nutrient solution remain constant. This substrate is very convenient for moving young plants, from the germination area to the growth area: move the whole cube with the roots delicately and place it directly in the hydroponic system. If you want to use the rock wool again, it is sufficient to wash it with bleach or Lysol in the 4: 1 ratio, then four parts of water and one of bleach or Lysol, then rinse and leave to dry.

Organic Cubes Root Riot

Root Riot cubes are composed of composted organic material. These cubes have a very spongy consistency and maintain the ideal oxygen/water ratio needed by plants in hydroponic cultivation. This material is used like traditional rock wool, and it is suitable both for cuttings and for seed germination. Generally, biodegradable sponge cubes are pre-fertilized (slightly) to improve the success rate of seed germination and the propagation of cuttings.

The peat

Peat is a soft and fluffy organic substance. It gets along very well with the roots of plants. It is often mixed with vermiculite, perlite (or agriperlite), and sand. It is good not to confuse peat for hydroponics with peat for soil. The color of the dry peat used in hydroponic cultivation is light brown; that of the soil is generally black. A defect of peat in hydroponics is that it becomes impermeable to water, once dry. Therefore it is advisable to keep it always moist even when not in use. A valid expedient may be to introduce it in hermetically sealed plastic bags. If you want to obtain a softer and draining substrate, you should follow one of these formulas:

10 liters of peat + 4 liters of perlite

10 liters of peat + 4 liters of vermiculite

10 liters of peat + 4 liters of expanded polystyrene into small pieces.

Expanded clay for horticulture

Expanded clay is an inert, non-organic, relatively light material widely used in hydroponic crops due to its properties: the expanded clay balls do not fit together, leaving ample spaces where oxygen accumulates. Expanded clay has excellent water retention and can absorb 30% of water as well as having, at the same time, a formidable draining power. It is reusable for many crops, sterilizes easily, and is recyclable. These qualities, combined with the fact of being economically convenient, have made it a perfect substrate for indoor hydroponic cultivation.

Perlite and Vermiculite

Perlite, or Agriperlite, and vermiculite are inorganic and inert materials. They are often used to lighten more compact substrates to make them airier and draining. In hydroponic cultivation, they are sometimes used alone or combined with portions of sand. They are light materials, generally packaged in bags in the form of granules or balls.

5. How many plants in a square meter?

Have you decided to embark on the adventure of indoor cultivation, but have little space? Have you already identified the place where you will place your plants, but you still don't know how many you can put in them? One of the most frequent questions among those who decide to start small indoor plant cultivation is "how many plants do I put in a square meter (10,76 square feet)?". The answer, of course, is it depends! Let's see, then, carefully what you need to know before starting small indoor home cultivation and how you can organize the plants within the space you have available.

The first consideration to make is related to the size and measurement of the areas to be used for cultivation. Some decide to carve out space inside a room, installing a complete grow box equipped with everything you need. Others instead have the opportunity to dedicate an entire room of the house to cultivation and create an ad hoc set-up with tools, the essential equipment, and accessories to create the ideal habitat for plants.

Once you have taken note of the exact dimensions of the space available, you will need to also and above all evaluate the necessary wattage of the lighting system and all the other useful equipment to be able to grow vigorous and healthy plants. The ideal number of plants per square meter can vary significantly from person to person, from the needs of cultivation, from the objectives to be achieved and from many other factors. We will, therefore, try to answer in an indicative way, to provide those who start today with the fundamental tools to start home cultivation.

So how many plants in a square meter?

The answer, as anticipated above, depends on the type of plants you intend to grow; usually, when they are large, the recommended number is one plant per square meter.

If, on the other hand, the plants are smaller, such as those of the salad, in particular, lettuce, which is one of the most frequently grown vegetables indoors, the recommended number is four per square meter. If they are even smaller in sizes, such as radishes or carrots, the number rises to sixteen per square meter.

There are also other types of plants, which are passionate about growers all over the world, for which particular considerations must be made, primarily based on the specific cultivation technique you choose.

The number of plants actually depends on the type of cultivation technique (in soil, hydroponics, or aeroponics). Generally, if the specimens are very small, it will be possible to grow from 4 to 9 plants per square meter. If they are little seedlings, you can go up to a maximum of 25, provided that certain precautions are followed, since the specimens will all be attached without leaving empty holes, thus creating a sort of "green sea." This technique - which allows you to optimize spaces to the maximum - is perfect for those who have a place with minimal dimensions. If, on the other hand, you want to get the most out of indoor cultivation, it is advisable to arrange 2 to 4 plants per square meter.

There is, then, another method that allows you to grow two plants per square meter in rather large pots, of 11 liters each, and is one of the best techniques for obtaining excellent results.

Grow Box 48"x48"x80" (120x120x200 cm): how many plants?

The number of plants that can be placed in a grow box naturally depends on their size. In a grow box measuring 48"x48"x80" (120x120x200 cm), or one of the most common sizes, for large plants, it is recommended not to go beyond 5-6 pots, for small plants. However, more pots can be added. In general, however, to be able to grow correctly, it is best not to exceed 8 plants.

In this case, the ideal light kit is the 600 watt one.

How many plants in a 24"x24" (60x60 cm) Grow Box?

One of the other most popular grow boxes is the small one, which measures 24"x24".

(60x60 cm); in this case, for a cultivation area measuring 24"x24" (60x60 cm) with a

height ranging from 55" to 75" (140 to 190 cm), the maximum recommended number of

pots is 4. By choosing this grow box, the ideal light kit is the 250 watt.

Useful tips

Generally, whatever the variety to be grown, it is not advisable to keep too-large plants inside indoor cultivation because, by requiring a more extended period for growth and development, the possibility of being subjected to attacks by insects and pests will tend to increase. Furthermore, the leaves of the too-large plants that are higher up will tend to absorb all the light at the expense of those below, which will thus tend to get sick.

Finally, it is good to remember that in indoor cultivation, just like those outsides, it is advisable always to keep everything clean and under control, and this is easier with small plants. With low-volume plants, it will be easier to identify an insect, a mold, a different color, and intervene in a timely and effective way to prevent the anomaly from spreading everywhere.

6. The importance to take care of the roots in DWC cultivation

A healthy and well-developed root system will make the plant grow better, contributing to the correct functioning of the system.

By growing plants with bare roots, the grower has the possibility of visually checking the state of health as well as the possibility of manually intervening on them.

It is possible, as well as recommended, to proceed with pruning the roots to promote lateral growth, the birth of new shoots, and avoid the occlusion of the connecting pipes.

In particular, it is advisable to do this using sterilized gloves and scissors, cutting only the tips and no more than 15% of the root. The cut parts must be removed and not left inside the system. Root pruning can be done during the 2nd week of growing and second time around the 2nd week of flowering.

To ensure the correct functioning of the system is vital to guarantee a natural flow of the solution between the vessels, it is necessary to check the growth of the roots periodically. In the case of occlusion of the tubes, remove them manually.

Root infection and rot

The diseases of the root system are often the consequence of incorrect management of the nutrient solution associated with inadequate cleaning of the equipment used.

There is no doubt that the best defense weapon is prevention, which consists of avoiding creating the ideal conditions for the development of bacteria and mold. The good news is that everything that will be done to counter the possibility of a bacterial infestation will do very well for the plant, which will be able to absorb the nutrients better and better counteract the diseases.

Among the leading causes of root rot, there are two diseases known as Phytium and Fusarium.

Trying to simplify, these diseases are the cause of the proliferation of a fungus whose spores usually are present in soils and waters. It thrives in humid environments, where there is poor oxygenation, attacking the roots of plants. It feeds on organic substances, blocking the ability to absorb nutrients and leading to the death of radical tissue.

If no action is taken in time, the roots of the plants attacked by Phytium will begin to take on a brownish color and, in a short time, to rot, releasing an unpleasant smell. At this point, the plant will stop absorbing the nutrients, the growth will be slowed down, the leaves will wither, and the production will consequently be limited.

Prevention

-Cleaning and sanitizing of the hydroponic system: at the end of each cultivation cycle, the system must be washed and sterilized to eliminate any form of pathogen present.

To disinfect the system, 35% hydrogen peroxide (H2o2) (3ml per liter) or bleach with a ratio of 1: 100 can be used.

Once the systcm has been completely emptied, remove the porous stones, and then fill it with water and a disinfectant.

At this point, turn on the pump and circulate the water inside the system for 2 or 3 hours, with the help of a sponge, rub and clean the cultivation pots thoroughly.

- Maintaining an optimal solution temperature: if the water temperature exceeds 70°F (21°C), the dissolved oxygen level decreases, and optimal conditions can be created for the development of pathogens and root rot. Always keeping the solution fresh with a temperature between 64°F and 70°F (18°C and 21°C) will help plants grow healthy and active.

- Frequent changes of the solution: changing the solution every 2 or 3 weeks is also useful to avoid any accumulation of zoospores responsible for problems with the root system.

- Cleaning of work tools: the cultivation room, as well as the equipment used, should always be cleaned and disinfected in this way to prevent bacteria and pathogens from being introduced into the cultivation.

-Fertilization: Fertilizers are not all the same! By using a quality product, the correct absorption of the elements present in the solution is guaranteed, and pH changes are avoided. The excess of fertilizers associated with constant changes in pH weakens the plant and makes it more vulnerable.

-Keep the correct environmental parameters of your cultivation room: when the light, temperature, and humidity of you.

7. How to take care of mother plants

What is cuttings reproduction, better known as cuttings? How to make cuttings? In this chapter, we will try to deepen the theme of the reproduction of plants. Any opportunity to understand how to increase the crop of plants must undoubtedly be carefully considered, and the development and maintenance of a mother plant is one of them. Taking care of a mother plant that ensures a large "renewable" crop is an excellent shortcut for successful cultivation. All this happens thanks to the cuttings that maintain the same genetic characteristics of the mother plant. The mother plants, therefore, guarantee the original stock, which allows many expert growers to maintain a quality harvest from their plants. However, for novices, these concepts about cutting can seem both very confusing and unnecessary work. We try to deepen the theme of reproduction by cuttings attempting to explain all the benefits that derive from having an excellent mother plant.

What is a mother plant?

A mother plant is a plant maintained perennially in the vegetative stage. Cuttings can be taken from this plant to create numerous genetically identical children that share precisely the same properties. If you want a continuous flow of abundant crops, easy to maintain, and quick to reach the end of the cycle, use these instructions, as the cuttings all come from the same stabilized plant and promise to replicate the same performance as the adult. Suddenly seed growth becomes much less attractive, being quite unpredictable and sometimes quite expensive - especially if rare and exotic plant varieties are involved!

How to select a mother plant?

If you have already grown a seed plant, you will know that even if the plants grow in the same environment, with the same substrate, with the same fertigation scheme, a small percentage of them will always end up with a less performing result. Some tend to sprout faster, some grow slower and thinner, and some seem a little strange. Nevertheless, the appearance of these plants may be completely different during flowering. Since the cuttings and clones must be made during the vegetative growth stage, it would be useful to do it for all the plants you intend to send in bloom. The important thing is to label both the cuttings and the plants from which they come to recognize them in the future.

The higher the number of plants from which you will take the cuttings, the higher the selection on the quality that you will then isolate. Many growers have finished their selection by identifying the plant with the best appearance at the initial stage of growth, but this selection can make us fall into error. The mistake derives from the fact that, at times, during the initial growth stage, a seedling can give disappointing results, excelling later during the flowering phase. Don't make the same mistake!

As soon as you have selected a cutting and elected it like your mother plant, you can eliminate the other candidates by sending them to bloom, leaving it time to develop.

What do you need to manage a mother plant?

Managing a mother plant is a relatively simple procedure that will precisely give the result you want to achieve by respecting the right times and paying due attention. Although indeed, this process is not difficult to follow, it is necessary to pay a little more attention rather than merely placing a light on the plant waiting for the shoots.

The mother plant needs a dedicated space (like a small grow box or a medium-size grow box) and a light source.

There is a wide choice to illuminate the mother plant. You can use neon lights, energy-saving lamps with a blue/white spectrum, or a metal halide discharge lamp. It is necessary to keep it on 18 hours a day to keep it in the vegetative stage. Although this type of lighting does not heat up too much, to maintain the optimal temperature in a smaller grow box, it is necessary to purchase an air extraction kit.

8. How to keep crops healthy

One of the most significant problems with hydroponic crops or any crops is the risk of disease or pests. Each of these can quickly destroy all the hard work and leave without a harvest.

That's why it's so important to know how to deal with these problems.

Disease

There are several ways in which the disease can manifest itself or be introduced into plants.

It is essential to be aware of what they are to prevent them from becoming a problem when growing crops.

Root disease

They are generally caused by a lack of oxygen that reaches the root of the plant, effectively causing them to rot. In a hydroponic system, the roots could always be in the water, increasing the risk of root disease.

However, as long as you keep the dissolved oxygen levels and keep the water moving, you shouldn't have any problems with root disease.

Wash your hands

Consider for a moment the number of different objects that we touch daily, and we will quickly have an idea of the amount of dirt and contamination that we can carry without realizing it, on our hands. This dirt, or bacteria, can be harmful to our plants, introducing bacteria that we cannot defend against.

To avoid this being a problem, it is necessary and advisable always to wash your hands or disinfect them before entering the cultivation space and managing the plants or the system. Shoes and clothes are equally important.

Disinfect the cultivation materials

A three percent bleach solution or three percent hydrogen peroxide solution is the best way to keep the growing environment clean. It is recommended to clean all equipment and surfaces with the solution after each harvest. This will prevent bacteria from reaching plants and potentially killing them.

No organic material

Hydroponic systems don't use soil, which is good because soil carries hundreds of different bacteria. Many of which can be harmful to plants.

However, just because we don't use the soil doesn't mean that soil contamination can't occur. It is always good to consider where the seedlings come from. If they were initially grown in the ground, they would need to be thoroughly cleaned before being planted in the culture media.

Keeping all soil and plant material away from the hydroponic system will help protect plants. It is better to grow from the seed instead of buying a seedling from the gardening shop.

Possible pests

Let's see below a list of potential pests. Here are some tips on how to get rid of it organically.

Aphids

These tiny black or sometimes green dots can quickly suck the goodness out of any plant. They walk along the stems and suck the sap from the plant. This removes the nutrients and will make the plant ill; eventually, it will die.

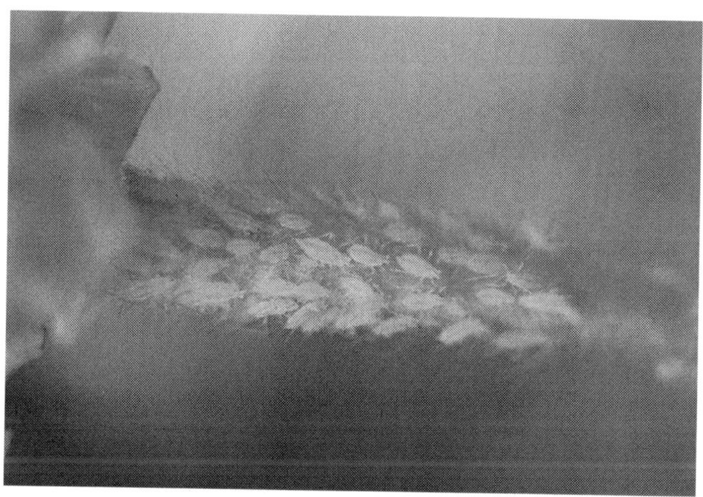

Some of the most commonly mentioned aphids are greenfly and blackfly. They can breed incredibly quickly. It is essential to treat them as soon as we find them; indeed, we don't want these pests spreading over to the rest of the crops.

Caterpillar

We already know what a caterpillar is. On its way to becoming a beautiful butterfly, it will chew through every green leaf it can find. On the plus side, these pests are relatively easy to pick off and remove; it's crucial to check the underside of your leaves where they usually hide.

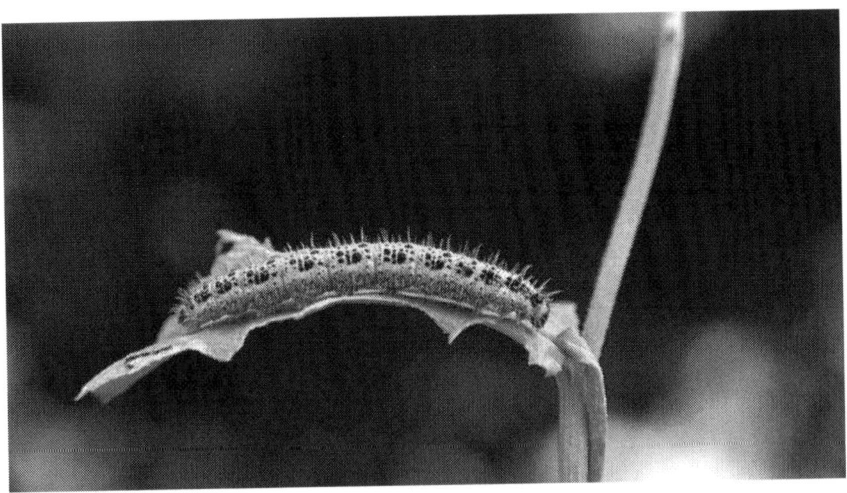

Squash Bugs

Unsurprisingly, these bugs are most commonly found on squash plants. They may not be an issue if we are not growing any squash. They look very similar to the stink bug, are approximately half an inch long, and have flatbacks. The squash bug is gray and brown with orange stripes on the bottom of their abdomen. We'll usually find them on the underside of the leaves in a group. They can fly but generally prefer to walk on the plants. These bugs will destroy the flow of nutrients to our plants.

Mealybugs

These are yet other pests that multiply quickly once they find a home. They tend to prefer warmer environments. The hydroponics setup will probably be ideal for their growth! The amount of damage they do will depend on the number of pests that are there; early detection is crucial. Mealybugs are oval insects approximately a quarter-inch long and covered with white or gray wax.

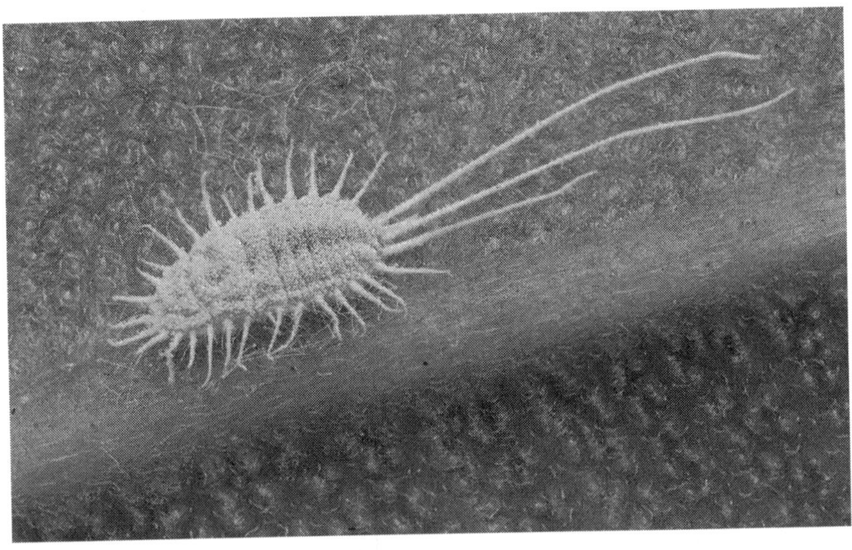

Cutworms

The cutworm is the larvae of several different species of adult moths. They will generally hibernate for the winter months; unless the hydroponic system is warm enough to discourage this. Once they finish hibernating, they will emerge and start eating the leaves of the plants. They generally feed at dusk; this is the best time to see them in action. They are effectively caterpillars but are often considered grubs. The exact size and look will depend on the species.

Hornworms

If there are tomatoes in hydroponics, it will be much easier to meet them! They are green, generally fat, and look like caterpillars. The adult moth lays eggs on the underside of your leaves in the late spring. These will hatch in less than a week. There will then have larvae, which will start to eat the plants for the next four to six weeks until nothing is left but the stems. They will generally go into a cocoon for the winter, but if the system is warm enough, they may only do this for a couple of weeks. They can then transform into moths and lay more eggs to feed on the plants. What might surprise is the size of the hornworm; it can be as much as five inches long! They are pale green and have white and black markings. They also have a horn at their rear, although this looks dangerous, they are not capable of stinging. It will be easy to find dark green droppings on the top of the leaves; this will tell we the hornworm is present; turn the leaf over to see them.

Dealing with pests

Having a greenhouse where soil-based plants are located is a bad idea. Pests could use the soil as a breeding ground before they move on to your hydroponics setup. Growing the produce from seed will drastically eliminate the possible pests that are on a plant. The plants buy from a local dealer could be filled with pests already.

Sap Suckers

One of the best natural remedies for sapsuckers is to spray the plants with chili or garlic spray. However, these can affect the taste of your crop and, in large quantities, can make it uncomfortable for the plants. Moderation is the key. Alternatively, we can use beneficial insects, that we'll talk about later.

Caterpillars

The simplest way of getting rid of caterpillars is to spray a substance called Bacillus Thuringiensis. It should be easy to buy it online or in the local garden store. It is a natural soil-borne bacteria that kills caterpillars and their larvae.

Mold & Fungus

Potassium bicarbonate is excellent at destroying virtually all molds and fungus. You can spray it directly onto any affected plants and the ones next to them.

Beneficial insects

Another great way of dealing with pests in your system is to use beneficial insects. As the name suggests, these are insects that will help our system by eating the pests that do damage. It is a good idea to have them in the system year-round. That means when there will be an outbreak, they might be able to limit it or negate the epidemic. Although it might not be easy to introduce them to the outdoor system, it is preferably done indoors or in a greenhouse where they are contained. It can be ordered online on sites like Amazon, insectsales.com, or a local organic gardening store.

Some of the best ones to consider are:

Ladybugs

These are great at getting rid of aphids before they can do any real damage. One ladybug can consume as many as five thousand aphids per year!

Parasitic Wasp

This tiny wasp doesn't sting. It will lay its eggs in the body of an aphid. The baby wasp eats the inside of the aphid before emerging to repeat the process.

Praying Mantis

These slightly strange looking creatures are excellent at eating aphids, caterpillars, potato beetles, leafhoppers, hornworms, squash bugs, and pretty much any pest that could be a problem for the system.

Lacewings

These are good at attacking virtually all types of pests. It is interesting to know that they are very good at eating aphids, mealybugs, whitefly, and even thrips. They can eat as many as one hundred aphids per week. They also work best at night when most of the pests are active.

It is worth noting that for a one thousand square foot greenhouse, you would need approximately two thousand lacewings. They can be taken from most biological insect vendors, or you can try planting flowers that attract lacewings near the system. Right flowers to plant are fennel, dill, coriander, dandelion, and angelica. They also like brightly-lit windows.

Spider Mite Predators

The tiny spider mite can suck the nutrients out of two hundred different plants. Fortunately, you can solve the issue by introducing the bright orange spider mite predator. They may only live for roughly forty-five days, but they can consume as many as twenty spider mites each day!

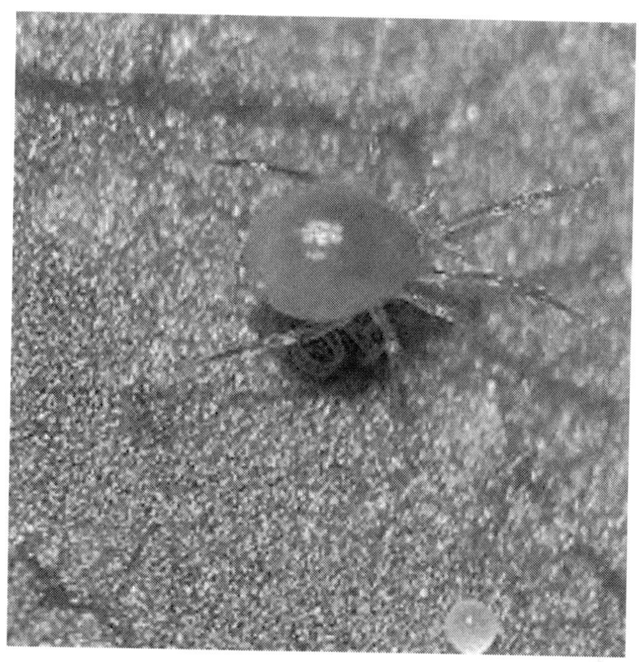

Aphid Predator Midge

These tiny little bugs look like small mosquitoes. They can sniff out aphid colonies, and then they lay their eggs next to them. Within a few days, the larva will hatch and eat the aphids. The aphid predator midge can consume as many as fifteen aphids a day.

Nematodes

These are natural parasites that are so small it can only see them with a microscope. They can kill approximately two hundred and fifty different types of larvae.

It is advisable to familiarize yourself with the most common pests in our area. Then it will be easier to deal with them!

9. PH in Hydroponic systems

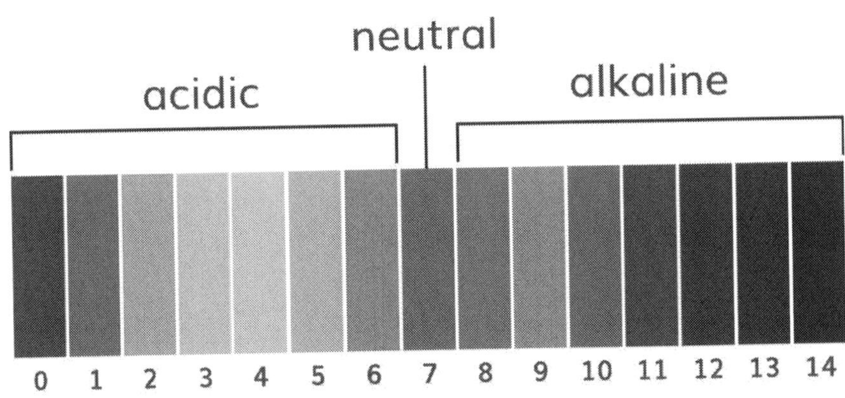

Balancing the pH in hydroponic crops is vital for the health and prosperity of your plants, especially as regards the harvest, the final result of months of waiting.

If the pH scale changes excessively, micro-elements and nutrients cannot be effectively absorbed by your plants as they are only available in solutions with an adequate pH range.

This can lead to nutrient deficiency and the possible death of your plants.

Definition of pH: what is it?

In chemistry, pH is a scale for measuring the acidity or basicity of an aqueous solution on a logarithmic scale in which 7 corresponds to a neutral value. As you can see from the scale shown in the graph above, which goes from 0 (which corresponds to the red color) to 14 (which coincides with the purple color), 0 corresponds to the acid value, while - on the opposite side of the scale - 14 corresponds alkaline value. Therefore, values less than 7 (i.e., all those values of the scale that oscillate between 0 and 7) are associated with more acid solutions, values greater than 7 (from 7 to 14) with more alkaline solutions.

Conventionally, the pH of aqueous solutions assumes values between 0 (maximum acidity) and 14 (maximum basicity/alkalinity). The neutral value, typical of pure water at 25 ° C, corresponds to the intermediate value of 7.

The pH can be measured electrically, exploiting the potential created by the difference in the concentration of hydrogen ions on two sides of a glass membrane (the pH meter is typical of this measurement), or chemically, exploiting the capacity of some substances (called indicators) to change their color according to the pH of the environment in which they are located.

Very often, the indicators are also used supported on strips of paper (the so-called "indicator papers"), which change color when immersed in acidic or basic substances.

The most common example is that of "litmus papers," pink in acid and blue in alkaline.

The pH of the soil decides which elements the plants will absorb

In indoor cultivation, many of the nutrient deficiencies visible on plants are often associated with the lack of nutrients in the substrate (coconut fiber, rock wool, soil, etc.) or in the nutrient solution that contains organic or mineral fertilizers. Still, what does not it is never considered, among the factors that trigger the criticality, it is the PH level of the soil and that relating to water.

Most of the time, the nutrients are already present in the substrate, but are not absorbed well by the roots due to the PH levels different from the optimal ones, and therefore recommended, which do not allow their absorption.

The only precise way to adjust the pH is to use a pH meter-tester or the pH indicator papers. Assumptions won't work

Specifically, it is necessary to measure the PH levels of the water or the nutrient solution which determines the absorption, by the plants, of the fertilizers dissolved in the liquid; therefore, for proper hydroponic cultivation, it is essential to have clear the optimal reference values are shown in the PH absorption table.

Not surprisingly, the pH influences the biological activity of some groups of microorganisms that exchange chemical elements (such as nitrogen, sulfur, iron, phosphorus, potassium, carbon, etc.) through the food chain interacting with the substrate they inhabit and releasing them elements ready to be absorbed by the roots.

Different species of plants have adapted to live at varying levels of absorbent pH, only useful nutrients. Still, we can say with certainty that the general level in the earth is estimated in a pH range between 6 and 6.8, slightly acidic. For hydroponic cultivation, however, the optimal pH range of the water is between 5.5 and 5.8. In this range, all plant nutrients are soluble in water so that plants quickly absorb them. Outside of this range, the ability of cultivated plants to absorb nutrients is less or zero.

Why is pH so important?

If the Ph of a substrate (in the specific case of hydroponic we speak of water) is outside the ideal range for cultivation, the plant loses the ability to absorb some of the nutrients essential for its growth, available only in solutions which show a specific pH range.

It should be known that the range of typical pH values can vary from plant to plant, generally preferring a slightly more acidic pH (lower than 7) although most plants can survive in a range between 5.0-7.5. In the case of a pH higher than 6.5, many nutrients and micronutrients separate from the solution and precipitate on the bottom of our hydroponic pot, thus making themselves unavailable for absorption by the plant, which will be adversely affected, because it is deprived of fundamental nutrients.

To avoid, therefore, that the plant goes into distress, it is of fundamental importance to make sure that the pH is in the correct range, and - if not - promptly correct it with appropriate solutions capable of raising or lowering it.

How to test the pH of our Hydroponic system

At this point, we know that balancing the Ph in hydroponic crops is vital to make nutrients available to our plants, but how can we control the values of our solution?

There are numerous options on the market, from the cheapest and least accurate to the most expensive and highly reliable.

The most economical option is to use a kit of papers which - once immersed in our solution - will change color depending on the type of pH detected. This color is then compared with a special reference table where the colors associated with the corresponding pH value are shown. These papers are generally disposable and inexpensive. However, they are very rough in determining the pH values of the solution.

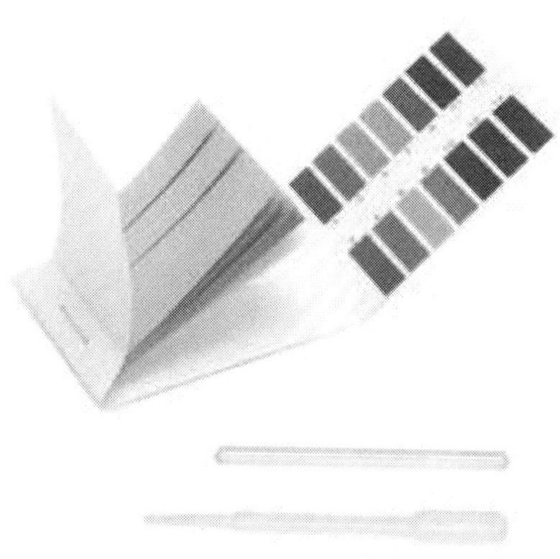

Another option for testing Ph levels is the use of liquid tests, which work with a color comparison method very similar to that of the papers: by adding a few drops of solution to the liquid test, the relative color appears after a few seconds. This is a somewhat known option given the higher accuracy in the interpretation of the result, remaining cheap.

As anticipated above, there are several tools for monitoring the pH levels of indoor crops. The most popular choice among hobbyists of indoor cultivation, however, is the digital pen, an extremely accurate meter (although it must be calibrated from time to time) that provides a digital reading of the pH values, by merely immersing the pen in the solution. These automatic meters are extremely accurate when calibrated regularly and can offer constant monitoring. Some of these are even able to take into account water temperature fluctuations that can influence the calculation of pH levels.

How to correct the pH levels of your Hydroponic solution

Once the pH measurement has been carried out, it will be necessary in most cases to adjust the values, using minimal quantities of pH + (pH up) or pH- (pH down) solutions according to our needs

PH levels should always be checked AFTER, adding nutrients to the solution as they tend to change its alkalinity or acidity.

The pH correctors can be dosed manually or using pumps specifically designed to continually keep the pH under control by releasing the acidic or alkaline solution to restore the correct values in case the probe connected to the pump and immersed in the hydroponic solution detects a pH out of the ideal range.

Organic lovers will be pleased to know that there are also totally BIO pH correctors on the market. This solution is far more expensive but also designed for those who do not want to leave anything to chance and want to keep the hydroponic system efficient without wasting too much time with measurements and any corrections/calibrations.

10. 8 Reasons to lower EC levels and eliminate chlorine from water

If we prefer a clean, quality environment and chlorine-free water (often bottled) for our drinking water, why should we not give our plants the same water? Even our plants DESERVE QUALITY WATER!

More nutritional substances for our plants

Plants can receive an electrical conductivity (EC) level of up to 1.4 to 2.2, depending on the type of plant or growth phase. For example, if the water we use already has an EC of 1.0, then we could only add 0.4 to 1.2 of nutrients (fertilizers) to reach our maximum levels. If, on the other hand, we start with an EC in the water of only 0.1 or 0.2 or even an EC of 0.0, then we will be able to add many more nutrients to our plants.

Healthy roots

By lowering the EC level, we eliminate the salts that we don't want in our water. This will give us healthier roots by avoiding the build-up of limescale, the roots and will be able to absorb 100% of the nutrients.

Keep a balanced pH

Using a reverse osmosis system to lower EC, we obtain a balanced pH of about 6.5.

Avoid the "nutrient lockout."

A high EC can contain large quantities of hard water minerals, such as calcium and magnesium, also known as limestone. High volumes of these minerals, together with additional doses of nutrients, can block or saturate the roots of plants by preventing them from absorbing the added nutrients, which is also known as "nutrient lockout."

Protect other microorganisms

Through the use of osmotic water, we can eliminate chlorine that would otherwise kill many specialized microorganisms.

Preventing problems

Many times, small or large issues are encountered during cultivation (yellowing, dry leaves, stunted growth, etc.), the cause of which often cannot be identified. By using an osmosis plant with a low level of EC, many of these problems can be avoided because we will have the opportunity to know exactly what nutrients and what quantities our plants are receiving.

Get better results from our nutrients

Starting with pure water, our plants do not absorb undesirable elements that may be present in the water. Therefore we will achieve 100% effectiveness in our addition of nutrients and fertilizers.

Pure water is fundamental for the healthy growth of plants

Just as a house needs to be built on a solid foundation, it needs to be flooded with purified water to have a solid foundation for growth. Irrigating with chlorine-free water with low EC levels is the right way to help our plants grow better!

How can I purify water and get chlorine-free water with EC at zero?

Through the reverse osmosis filters connected to the water network, you will have the opportunity to obtain perfect water for your plants.

11. How to optimize cultivation using led lamps

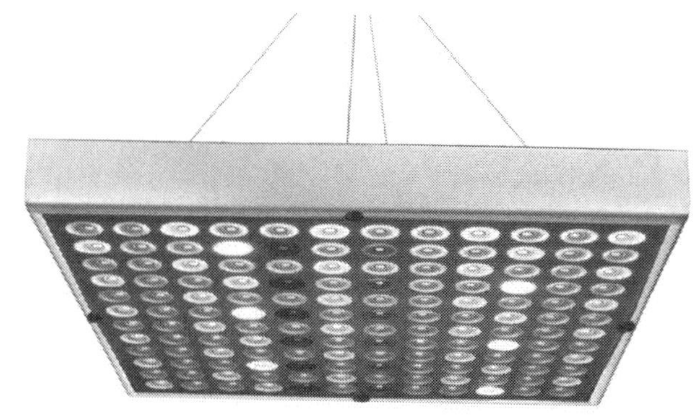

Hydroponic growers in the 21st century have different options than hydroponic growers of a generation ago. One of the most recent and most exciting developments is the introduction of LED lights for hydroponics. These lights allow not only to give larger yields and faster harvests but also to cause less damage from too much heat and bring some relief when paying the electricity bill. If you decide to switch to this cultivation method, you will not be able to use the same techniques used with halogen or high-pressure sodium lamps. At the same time, most of the skills you have acquired as a hydroponic cultivator are transferable. Growing with LED lights, some unique conditions require special instructions. By following these simple steps, you can be sure of getting the most out of growing by using LED lights.

Do not allow your Grow Room to become cold

If you live in a rather cold part of the world, you may have used the heat that comes from traditional lamps to keep cultivation at an optimal temperature. Once you switch to the LED, you will notice a noticeable drop in temperature, which may mean that you will need to purchase a heater connected to a thermostat to keep the grow room warm enough. Don't worry, though. Even if you have to use additional equipment, by using the best of the LED, you will still have a net saving of electricity.

Be careful not to water too much

You may have spent a lot of time finding the optimal conditions for watering the plants. Many believe that after switching to LED lights, the irrigation regiment itself leads to overloads, which is since lower heat levels cause less evaporation of water. After starting to use LED lights, be sure to find signs of overexposure. If you suspect that the roots of the plants are suffering, you can try leaf-feeding so that the plants get enough nutrients while correcting the problem.

Don't be afraid to bring the lights closer

The closer the lights get, the more intense the light will be for the plants. If in the past, you have used lamps with particularly high heat production, you may have some hesitation about the lighting of the plants. Still, since the heat production of the LEDs is significantly lower, you can feel free to experiment and put the lights closer than before. Increased intensity can increase photosynthetic activity and plant growth. You also need to make sure to place the lights closer when using a CO2 generator as higher concentrations of carbon dioxide mean greater demand for nutrients and light.

12. How to lower the temperature of the Grow Room

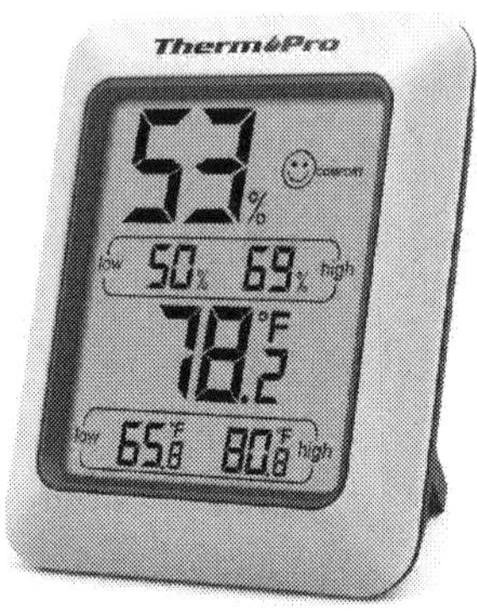

The temperature in the grow room is a critical parameter to monitor and regulate.

The ideal temperature is 79°F (26°C); the optimal temperature range is between 70°F and 82°F (21°C and 28°C).

The temperature must be monitored through simple measuring instruments such as thermometers or thermo-hygrometers.

There are several models, but we recommend using a digital thermometer with the Min / Max function, which allows you to know the current temperature and also the minimum and maximum temperature reached during a specific period.

In this way, we can see if the temperature has exceeded the recommended values. Below we see what to do if we find that we have exceeded the recommended maximum temperatures.

Air system

To decrease the temperature in a grow room, we can use an extractor fan or air extractor. The extractor positioned at the top sucks in the hot air, so the heat will tend to drop. A thermostat can control the aspirator in order to operate in the hottest hours, which are generally those in which the lighting system is on; in fact, when the lights are off, there is a decrease in temperature. Place an axial aspirator in the lower part of the grow box / grow room (of lower power than the aspirator at the top) to push the fresh air inside the grow. In this way, air circulation is guaranteed

Lighting system

Most growers use HPS lamps for flowering, i.e., they illuminate with high sodium pressure bulbs. The problem with these lamps is the high temperature they produce, especially in summer. A CoolTube reflector can be a convenient solution to decrease the temperature of the lights by at least 41°F (5°C).

In recent years users of LED lamps are spreading. The led light is a plate of many small diodes, of very few watts each, of the right color. The drawback of this technology is the poor penetration of the LEDs, but with a Scr.O.G. well-measured, you get a decent harvest even when the outside temperature exceeds 86°F (30°C). An ideal solution for indoor growing even in August!

Air-conditioning the growing area

If the extraction system combined with that of the lights is not sufficient to keep the temperature under control, consider using an air conditioner more. If you have an air conditioner in your home, you can use it to cool the surrounding air, which will be pushed into the grow box by the extractor fan. If you have a medium-sized grow room, you can consider purchasing a portable air conditioner.

Products to help plants cope with the heat

To protect and help plants in conditions of thermal stress, it is possible to use products that cool or fortify plants by hydrating them. They help plants thrive when the temperature exceeds 86°F (30°C), reinforce them against heat stress, and prevent the abortion of flowers in unfavorable conditions.

13. How to fight odors in the Grow Box

One of the most important aspects, when we talk about indoor cultivation, is undoubtedly the air treatment in the grow boxes. Among the problems that emerge in this area, one of the most delicate to deal with is that of the smells generated inside them.

In fact, inside the grow rooms, there is a constant flow of hot air rich in humidity and various smells. Each of us subjectively perceives these odors; consequently, those that are pleasant to us for others could be annoying; it is, therefore, advisable to eliminate them so as not to run into neighborhood problems.

How to eliminate unpleasant odors in the Grow Box

Among the various solutions to eliminate odors inside the grow box, we find:

- Activated carbon filters

- Gel or spray anti-odor treatment

- Ozonizers to reduce odors and purify the air

Among these solutions, the one most used is undoubtedly that of activated carbon filters. One of their advantages is convenience; they are already predisposed to be hooked to the air exhausters through flexible ducts to convey the flow to the outside.

These filters are made up of activated carbon with chemical processes and retain most of the volatile molecules (about 95% of the organic molecules). Activated carbon filters are incredibly porous and have a high number of active sites per unit of volume, but, after a specific time, they saturate and must be replaced. The replacement time of the activated carbon filters depends on the size of the grow room and the number of volatile molecules present.

A parameter to be carefully checked to evaluate the effectiveness of activated carbon filters is the humidity in the cultivation chamber. Plants prefer a humidity rate of 70% RH; with this rate, the effectiveness of activated carbon is lower. The solution for growers who want to obtain a perfectly odor-free grow box will be to integrate with an anti-odor gel/spray treatment or with an ozone generator or both.

The anti-odor treatments in gel or spray neutralize persistent odors by releasing pleasant aromas depending on the chosen fragrance. They contain a complex natural formula of essential oils based on terpenes, bio-molecules present in the resins of many plants. Once released into the air, they can attract and replace the molecules of any odor of organic origin with their pleasant scent.

The last solution mentioned to prevent or take action on odors in the grow box is related to the ozone generator. These produce negative ions and combine them with ozone to eradicate volatile and polluting organic gas molecules such as pollen, dust, cigarette smoke, and even vaporized substances as propellants for aerosols and car vapors. In high concentrations, the ozone can be toxic, and therefore the utmost attention is recommended and check that the ozone generator is turned off before entering the grow box.

To conclude, the best advice to achieve our goal is to use all the elements we have available because only in this way can we be reasonably sure of definitively eliminating odors from our grow box without more or less unpleasant residues.

14. How to grow in Hydroponics in summer

The problems of Hydroponics in summer:

Summer, especially when it is very hot, can become a difficult season for hydroponics growers.

The higher the temperature, the less oxygen remains in the nutrient solution and in the summer when the external or internal temperature reaches 86°F (30°C) and even 104°F (40°C), you must start to worry.

With high temperatures and little oxygen available, the roots begin to deteriorate, and in a short time, pathogenic organisms such as fungi and aggressive parasites develop. We consider that for most plants, the ideal solution temperature should fluctuate between 59°F and 73°F (15°C and 23°C). So to face the heatwave of summer, you can take different ways, all valid according to the need and the economical possibility. Below we see some of them:

Water coolers

The water chillers (Chillers) use refrigerant gas to cool the water that passes inside them; they are low-noise and equipped with controllers to set the desired temperature. The water chillers guarantee the maintenance of the set temperature in hydroponic systems or in aquariums. They are very useful in cooling tank water.

Additional oxygenators

Integrate porous stones with oxygenators by increasing the oxygenation of the nutrient solution. The higher the oxygenation, the greater the chances of maintaining a proper temperature/oxygen ratio.

Special fertilizers

To protect and help plants in conditions of thermal stress, it is possible to use products that cool or fortify plants by hydrating them. Products like Chill or Liquid Ice help plants thrive when the temperature exceeds 86°F (30°C). They strengthen plants against heat stress and prevent the abortion of flowers in unfavorable conditions.

Useful tips for dealing with the problems of Hydroponic cultivation in summer

In conclusion, if you are fighting against the summer heat or in general with high temperatures, follow the following tips:

- Check plant roots often, use silicate powders to prevent fungus infestation

- Check that there are no harmful insects, even the smallest spider or aphid specimen. If a plant doesn't look right, check the roots, but if it's sick, throw it away

- Change the water as regularly as possible

- Keep the electrical conductivity low to avoid excessive salt absorption.

15. How to grow in Hydroponics in winter

How to prepare our Grow Room for winter

Are cold winter nights coming and low temperatures with them?

It is time to start thinking about the temperature in our grow room to keep our plants, especially their roots, warm and comfortable.

This is particularly important when growing with hydroponic systems since unlike soil or coconut substrates, which offer the roots a certain degree of thermal insulation, the water used in hydroponics does not thermally insulate.

First of all, our grow room must be well thermally insulated. Adding heat through a heater will not make much difference if the hot air is dispersed and does not remain inside the grow box. When we use a grow box (Grow Box), it is ideal to place it on a mat rather than in contact with the cold floor. We can also use insulating materials generally used for construction because if they can insulate a house, let alone a grow box!

Idea: Instead of placing potted plants or tanks in contact with the floor, let's put them on inverted pots. This helps to distance the bases of your hydroponic vessels and not from the cold floor.

Let's change the lighting hours

HID lamps can cause problems in the summer due to the heat they produce.

We use this to our advantage by illuminating the Grow Room during the evening/night hours when the environment tends to be less hot and temperatures generally colder, instead of turning off the lights during the day.

The heat produced by the lamps will help counteract the frost of the night. If the plants are still in the vegetative phase when winter arrives, growers should consider extending the lighting hours from 18 to 20/22, if not 24 hours.

We use secondary heaters

The heat produced by our lamps, especially if LEDs are used, may not be sufficient to ensure the ideal temperatures in our cultivation environment. Therefore, a secondary heater is necessary.

Designed explicitly for grow boxes, the heating pipes are small enough to be placed at any height inside the tent. They offer optimal performance with absolutely marginal consumption; in fact, they can release constant heat into the surrounding air, keeping the grow box at a stable temperature.

Heater tubes do not have a temperature control but can easily be combined with a thermostat.

How to use the Grow Box heater tube?

The use of the heater tube is effortless to program. All you need is a power outlet and an analog timer.

We recommend placing the tube away from liquids, ensuring that the outer edges of the heater do not come into contact with external materials, such as curtain fabric, plastic or plant material.

A useful strategy for getting the most out of your heater during the colder months is to schedule the heater to turn on when the lights on the indoor system go off at the beginning of the dark hours. The heater will provide enough heat to maintain the ideal temperature in the dark range.

Duct heaters

The second option is the use of duct heaters. However, they must be used with caution because the dry and humid air introduced could easily cause a decrease in humidity, damage plants or prevent their growth if directly projected onto our loved ones. Our recommendation is to use duct heaters only in the areas surrounding the Grow Box to heat the air, or positioned towards the cold air inlet. Certainly to avoid is that the heater is directed towards the plants.

Thermo-fan Ceramic heater

A third option, for more spacious rooms, is the use of a ceramic heater with air fan for a correct distribution of the heated air.

Its use makes it possible to heat large rooms (up to 30 square meters) with reduced consumption.

Equipped with switch and thermostat, it is ideal for maintaining the desired temperature.

Let's check the suction

If you are introducing air from the outside into the grow box, you are also bringing the cold inside, making it challenging to keep your plants at an optimal temperature.

In this case, you can position your aspirator so as to introduce the air from the surrounding room into the grow box rather than from the outside. Another advantage in sucking air from indoor environments is that it also adds a higher amount of CO_2. Control units can also be used, both for extraction and aspiration. These monitor temperatures and consequently adjust the suction and expulsion of air from the grow box.

During the vegetative phase and at the beginning of flowering, lowering the air extraction level by a few percentage points would allow the hot air to remain longer in the grow box, at the same time, refreshing the environment often enough to allow our plants to grow healthy and luxuriant. However, this may not be an option in the case of a more advanced flowering phase, since the odors would require the extractor to operate continuously at full capacity. In this case, then, we should consider a secondary heater.

We check the temperature of the nutrient solution

When we prepare our solution, especially if in large quantities with the nutrients stored for a certain number of days, it is vitally important that the temperature of the solution fluctuates between 64°F and 70°F (18°C and 21°C). If the temperature drops too low, the roots of the plants could be affected, slowing down the absorption of nutrients and, in some cases, going into shock, preventing their growth. On the contrary, at too high temperatures, the solution would contain a lower level of oxygen, the lack of which would slow down growth or make the plant more susceptible to diseases such as fungi and root rot. To prevent this from happening, we often check the solution temperature and use a solution heater to keep it at the optimum temperature. Designed to be completely immersed in water, they can maintain the solution at the temperature we have chosen at all times.

Idea: We often check the solution with an immersion thermometer that can be used to monitor the temperature of liquids, which can be immersed in the solution to give us an accurate reading at all times.

Last but not least: we continuously monitor

Plants grow lush at temperatures between 77°F-82°F (25°C-28°C) when the lighting is on and 64°F-70°F (18°C-21°C) with the illumination off, so it is essential to monitor often the air conditions in the grow box to make sure that these parameters remain constant.

Simply, we pay attention to temperatures and humidity using a digital thermometer to allow us to act promptly if some adjustment is needed.

The most significant advantage of having an indoor hydroponic system is that it allows us to grow our plants all year round. However, this does not mean that they are safe from low winter temperatures. These simple tricks will ensure optimal results, regardless of outside temperatures and seasons.

16. Organic Hydroponics

Can Hydroponic cultivation be organic?

Usually, the fertilizers for hydroponic cultivation are of the "mineral" type and are generally produced with refined salts and entirely soluble in water (rich in chelates).

They have been deprived of heavy metals and pollutants.

A mineral hydroponic fertilizer, if it is a high-quality product, is designed to not leave any trace of toxicity in your plants, provided you follow the recommendations for use and the correct dosage.

For years we have tried to combine the advantages of hydroponic cultivation with those of organic agriculture on the ground, but always with negative results precisely because the specific fertilizers for hydroponics, being minerals, are, in fact, non-organic.

The goal of Bioponica is to create hydroponic cultivation that uses only organic fertilizer made up of fertilizers that are perfectly soluble in water and do not clog irrigation systems. Bioponics is a revolutionary cultivation method that allows you to make hydroponic cultivation that is 100% organic.

Create liquid earth

The concept of bioponic is to recreate liquid earth with the advantages of hydroponic cultivation. To be bioponic, fertilizer must be liquid or completely soluble. It must not contain too large particles and must be rapidly degradable and available.

17. How to make a natural fertilizer at home

One of the main advantages of hydroponics is the ability to carefully and accurately control both the life cycle of plants and their development. Elements such as humidity, light, and nutrients must remain constant and well balanced. In this way, the plants will grow vigorous, robust, and the vegetables will mature in a luxuriant way. There are a variety of fertilizers, including natural ones, which guarantee plants the right amount of mineral salts and nutrients.

The substances that must never be missing for the development of the plant are:

Nitrogen;

Phosphorus;

Potassium;

Football;

Magnesium

These substances are essential both during the vegetative and development phase of the plant. In addition to these crucial nutrients, other fundamental nutrients must be added to fertilizers, which vary according to the type of plant, but also according to the phase of the life and development cycle in which they are found.

Here they are listed below:

Manganese;

Iron;

Sulfur;

Zinc;

Boron;

Molybdenum

It is essential - when creating a home fertilizer - to use organic nutrients in pure form since with commercial fertilizers, this is not always obvious.

The plant needs 3 essential nutrients, nitrogen, phosphorus, and potassium, but it also requires 10 other elements, such as sulfur, magnesium, calcium, iron, manganese, zinc, copper, chlorine, boron and molybdenum. It is imperative to calibrate the proportions between these components to make plants grow optimally and keep an eye on the PH level. For this reason, both amateurs and professionals usually opt for ready-to-use solutions, but this does not exclude the possibility of creating a proper fertilizer at home.

Nitrogen has beneficial effects on plant growth, and it helps in the development of the woody part, leaves, stems, and branches. Phosphorus is never pure, at least in nature, but by combining it with oxygen, it gives life to phosphorus pentoxide, very important for the development of fruits and tissues. Potassium, on the other hand, helps in the absorption of the different elements and micronutrients.

The most common homemade nutrients are based on fertilizer salts. Although the disadvantage of this technique is that you have to buy many and at a fairly high price; for this reason, it is advisable to purchase ready-to-use fertilizers, which guarantee high quality at the best price.

There are, however, a variety of salts to choose from at different prices and for all budgets, although it is always advisable to select those that, although they have a higher rate, have more excellent solubility and longer life.

Potassium chloride, for example, is used more than potassium sulfate; however, if it is applied for more than a few days, the chlorine present in the mix could prove harmful to plants. Magnesium nitrate can be replaced with magnesium sulfate, but it is rare to replace it, as magnesium sulfate (Epsom) costs much less. As mentioned above, in addition to the three main elements, plants also need those essential ten elements. There are many nutritional formulas to inspire. The important thing is that the elements are always used in balanced quantities, although it is still very complex to choose the best formula.

Plants need different nutrients based on the days and at different times of the day, so it is very complex to determine what plants need, at least not to do complete tests every day. When preparing fertilizers yourself, it is advisable to provide the plant with a natural and balanced nutrient solution all the time. With the term balanced, it is meant to give the plant the right ratio of elements to meet the maximum requirements of the plant. The rate is usually determined by calculating the parts per million concentration of each element.

The plant absorbs what it needs through the small hairs at the ends of its roots. This process makes it impossible to overfeed it in hydroponic crops. However, care must always be taken when mixing the concentration of nutrients in the water, because an excessive amount would compromise the ability of the plant to absorb water. If the salts are diluted in too high a concentration, the plant will release the water instead of consuming it, leading to dehydration.

To get started, you need to purchase the following items:

- 280 grams of sodium nitrate
- 280 grams of calcium nitrate
- 280 grams of potassium sulfate
- 425 grams superphosphate
- 140 grams of magnesium sulfate

The underlying trace elements will be mixed in a separate container:

- 28 grams of iron sulfate
- 1 teaspoon of manganese sulfate

- 1 teaspoon of boric acid powder

- 1/2 teaspoon of zinc sulfate

- 1/2 teaspoon of copper sulfate

The ingredients are mixed thanks also to the use of the pestle and mortar which transform the largest substances into powder; as a general rule, a ratio of ½ teaspoon per 100 liters of water must be used, and it is recommended not to leave leftovers since it is not possible to reuse them after 24 hours. During the vegetative phase, the nitrogen content must be high, while the quantities of potassium and phosphorus must be medium-high. Once the flowering period has started, the nitrogen percentages will have to decrease, while the potassium and phosphorus percentages will have to increase.

Another do-it-yourself and natural fertilizer is seaweed: a sort of tea is prepared in which algae will be immersed, which will have to ferment a few days near sunlight; you will then need to add 1 teaspoon of Epsom salt for each liter of liquid and mix the solution in the feed tank. It is always important to check the PH levels so that the values remain around 5.5 and 6.5.

Another fertilizer to be able to do alone is that with food waste, for example, it is possible to create other teas with organic material, such as earthworm wraps, eggshells, and bat guano. With this procedure, it is also advisable to add vitamin B in the form of tablets, which help the flowering of the plant: it will be sufficient to crush the tablets with a mortar and pestle and then insert them in the feeding tank.

Another way to create natural fertilizer at home is to use banana peels, rich in potassium, which helps to strengthen the plants during the plant's nutritional phase. To make the most of the potential of banana peels, just put them in a container full of water, let them macerate for about 24 days, and then use the water for irrigation.

To conclude some practical tips to create your natural fertilizer:

Store fertilizer salts, trace elements and nutrients in airtight containers, away from moisture;

When preparing nutrients, it is essential to use a large, clean bowl for mixing. The crystals will be crushed with a mortar and a pestle (the type of the pharmacy is the best);

Grind the trace elements separately and add the latter, mixing everything very carefully; it is important to ensure that the powders are completely dissolved in water before application to the hydroponic system. Many times later, adjustments will be needed to create your ideal fertilizer, and this is probably the most challenging part of hydroponics. The various changes will have to be made with caution; otherwise, the inside will be damaged. To be sure of using the right combinations and the correct doses of fertilizers, it is always advisable to turn to ready-made and packaged products, where the aseptic conditions and the adjustment of the variables - indispensable elements for optimizing production - are guaranteed.

18. Vertical Garden: vertical Hydroponic and Aeroponic systems to cultivate indoor

The vertical hydroponic and aeroponic systems are designed to optimize space and yield for large-scale crops.

This type of system is particularly suitable for use in the new kind of green farm, The Vertical Farm, which develops vertically, a symbol of green agriculture, with zero impact.

If applied and spread on a large scale, this type of agriculture, thanks to the use of innovative hydroponic systems for crops and vertical gardens, could truly change the fate of the planet and improve the living conditions of entire communities around the world. Even by applying it to small businesses, such as domestic and family, vertical cultivation with hydroponic systems allows you to start thriving crops, allowing families to save on daily food shopping and always to have fresh food available.

These hydroponic systems for vertical cultivation are ideal for those who have little space and do not have the opportunity to carve out a space for the creation of a traditional horizontal vegetable garden.

These systems for vertical hydroponic cultivation are also called vertical greenhouses or hydroponic towers, precisely because they allow you to cultivate any vegetable in very little space freely. These towers, in fact, can be placed in a small greenhouse, in a garden, in a garage, or even in a small room in the house.

What is it, and where to create it: vertical indoor or outdoor garden?

Very popular in recent times, especially in the most avant-garde and particularly environmentally friendly European countries, the vertical garden is a setting that houses compositions of different plants inserted in special pots and anchored on special panels, or attached directly to the internal wall. or building exterior. Vertical gardens adapt to any environment: indoors and outdoors, such as private rooms, rooms in homes and residences, offices, open spaces, and all other types of public premises.

Typical examples of internal vertical gardens are those installed in homes, for example in entrance halls of condominiums, in correspondence with a very long wall, or a dividing wall between two different rooms of the house; however, they adapt very well both to rooms intended for study and work and in kitchens. Among the most common examples of vertical outdoor gardens, however, we find those created to embellish and decorate entire facades of buildings, dividing and containment walls, fences, self-supporting walls, or separating panels of any type and on any structure.

But how do you keep plants in vertical greenery?

The cultivation method adopted for vertical green is the classic one, with a base of potting soil irrigated with water by means of a simple sprayer, or alternatively, the drop-shaped hydroponic one, installed in the upper part of the panel or wall, where, instead of universal soil, an inert substrate is adopted (composed for example of coconut fiber, perlite, expanded clay, etc.) and the irrigation water is enriched with nutrients and fertilizers capable of feeding the plants.

There are also other solutions, always based on hydroponic systems, which allow adapting to various surfaces and different types of supports. It is possible to choose between multiple types of hydroponic gardens, also known by the name of green or vertical green walls, adaptable according to the various needs.

Vertical Garden: What are the benefits?

In addition to embellishing the environment with the colors of nature and making the spaces more welcoming and aesthetically more attractive, the preparation of vertical green space of this type also allows you to purify the air and make it purer, thus lowering the levels of pollution of the environment.

The plants absorb the Co2, or the carbon dioxide present in the air, thus generating cleaner air and also ensuring thermoregulation.

But there is more because if the vertical garden is located outside, the plants are also able to absorb UV rays and clean the air from the smog generated by cars and nearby polluting buildings.

Furthermore, vertical gardens can offer excellent thermal and acoustic insulation, creating a natural protective barrier capable of improving the quality of life of the people living in that space.

Furthermore, thanks to this action of insulation and insulation, also of a thermal type, the vertical green wall can lower the need and energy consumption, both for heating and for cooling, and consequently also allows economic savings. Without forgetting that a green panel gives relaxation, because, thanks to the colors and scents of nature, it helps to rest the eye, it helps to relax the mind and even increase the value and charm of the property.

Which plants to choose for the Vertical Garden?

The selection and choice of plants to be used in the vertical garden naturally varies both according to the climatic and environmental characteristics of the area in which they are installed (such as exposure of the house, ventilation, etc.) and from personal preferences and individual needs. For example, depending on your preferences, you can choose climbing plants, which naturally will develop very high, or cascade plants, which grow downwards; alternatively, it is possible to opt for small evergreen plants, or those with limited growth, in order to guarantee a reduced commitment and a low level of maintenance.

For the kitchen or for the more recreational environments of the house, it is also possible to create a space to dedicate to vertical greenery populated by aromatic herbs, such as rosemary, lavender, sage and citron grass, which, in addition to ensuring the presence of a pleasant green composition to the eye, they also spread relaxing and beneficial scents and aromas for a unique experience, capable of significantly improving the quality of life.

In general, the plants most used for creating vertical gardens are ferns, philodendron, ficus, and fatsia japonica, because they are very resistant and can live even in particularly difficult conditions.

More and more people are turning to vertical crops, both to experiment with new types of agriculture and for space needs.

19. Idea: 25 types of herbs, vegetables, and ornamentals to grow in Hydroponics

We have selected 20 types of plants for hydroponics, easy to grow in water, and with adequate lighting. Most of these are well known to you if you love to make a vegetable garden, but perhaps you don't know that they can be grown even without land.

Vegetables

Different tasty vegetables can be grown inside a water and nutrient substrate comfortably indoors. Some are common vegetables that you would typically grow in your garden, and others are a variety especially suitable for growing in smaller spaces:

Bok Choy (photo)

Lettuce

Spinach

Tomato

Sweet pepper

Cucumber

Celery

For the support of larger plants (like tomatoes), you prefer clay pebbles to give the roots a firmer grip.

Aromatic and medicinal herbs

Many people love to create a small corner of the house or on the balcony dedicated to aromatic herbs, planting them in earthen pots or setting up a simple vertical vegetable garden. Growing fresh herbs in hydroponics is an easy way to try this technique before moving on to other types of plants.

If you intend to try to grow one of these plants, start from a cutting rather than seeds.

This not only makes the plant stronger but also faster to grow. Here is what you can choose for your hydroponics:

Origan

Basil

Rosemary

Sage

Stevia

Tarragon

Peppermint

Spearmint

Melissa

House plants

Finally, here are some ideal houseplants to grow without land and quickly enough in a hydroponic system.

You know many of them, and you have already grown them with other methods: why not take a cutting and cultivate them in hydroponics? Houseplants are not only beautiful to have, but they also help to clean the air by absorbing carbon dioxide during the day.

Potos

Syngonium (Syngonium)

Philodendron (Philodendron)

Spatafillo

Coin plant (Pilea peperomioides)

Dragon tree

Dieffenbachia

Falangio

Aglaonema

Which of these hydroponic plants will you try to grow?

20. How to deal with the most common problems

It feels great to get your hydroponic system set up and established, especially as the crops start to appear. However, it is essential to maintain the environment and keep an eye out for some of the most common problems.

If you catch them fast enough, you will be able to react quickly and save the plants.

Common deficiencies in hydroponics:

-Calcium

-Magnesium

-Iron

Other problems include:

-Chlorosis - Yellowing of the leaves

-Necrosis - Death of the leaf

Nitrogen deficiency (N)

Yellow leaves can be a sign of a nitrogen deficiency. If nitrogen deficiency occurs, the plant will move the available nitrogen from the older leaves (bottom) to the new leaves (top). This means the bottom leaves will become yellow while the top leaves are still green. If you scrutinize the leaves, you will see that the yellowing begins at the tip of the leaves, slowly making it's way to the center.

Phosphorus deficiency (P)

The leaves become darker, almost purple. The leaves will start to curl and will eventually drop. Phosphorus will be hard to spot at the beginning.

Potassium deficiency (K)

Potassium deficiency is also hard to spot. Older leaves (bottom) will form chlorosis (yellowing), and the edges of the leaf will turn brown with sometimes brown spots in the middle of the leaf.

The flowering of the plant is greatly diminished.

Calcium deficiency (Ca)

Calcium deficiency appears on new leaves. The edges of the leaf turn brown. Calcium deficiency is not to be confused with tip burn (too many nutrients) or lack of airflow.

It might be possible that your plants are developing signs of calcium deficiency even when there is enough calcium in the nutrient solution. This is because the environment you are growing in is too humid. The leaves cannot transpire water, which will lead to less nutrient uptake. One of these nutrients that fails to be taken up is calcium. Calcium is used to maintain cells. If calcium is not supplied, the new leaves will turn brown on the edges.

Decrease the humidity to fifty percent and install fans to circulate the air.

Magnesium deficiency (Mg)

Deficiencies can exist four weeks before you could see it happen. The leaves at the bottom will start to yellow between the veins (interveinal yellowing) with brown spots forming on the leaves. Over time, the leaves will almost completely turn white.

The older leaves will dry and curl up, eventually falling off the plant.

Iron deficiency (Fe)

Iron deficiency will lead to interveinal chlorosis at the new leaves (top). If you are using UV lights to remove algae from the water, you may have an iron deficiency. UV light makes iron precipitate out of the solution, making it unavailable for your plants to take up.

Too many nutrients

Too many nutrients can become a problem when you have nutrient build-up or just have added too many nutrients.

As previously mentioned, you do not want to give seedlings a full dose of nutrients. You should provide them with a quart or half of the dose of the mature plant.

Too many nutrients will result in a nutrient burn, which is brown spots at the edge of the leaves. Not to be confused with calcium deficiency. The leaves will become dark green and start to curl up.

If your plants have a nutrient burn, you need to flush them with a half-strength solution and lower the nutrient concentration.

21. Hydroponics as a form of extra income

With a little space available, time, and know-how, you can easily add a few hundred euros a month to your bank account. This is possible if you grow vegetables for the neighborhood or to supply some local fruit and vegetable shops. You certainly won't get rich from hydroponics in your garden, but it will undoubtedly be fun and exciting.

First of all, you have to consider what kind of plant you want to grow. Each plant requires the right set up of the hydroponic system. For example, strawberries grow well in the NFT system, tomatoes in the low nitrogen concentration DWC system, and cucumbers in the high nitrogen concentration DWC system.

We advise you to start with a small space and set up a small hydroponic system to get practical with hydroponic cultivation. Try to grow seasonal fruit and vegetables to facilitate the sale. The final product will be of excellent quality and also the yield will be higher than the traditional cultivation in the ground.

Once ready, expand your system and start your intensive hydroponic cultivation. You will see that your friends and customers will thank you because the product will be of quality.

If instead of leaving the hydroponic system outdoors, you can close it or bring it indoors, with the help of artificial light, you will be able to grow all year round. By growing off-season products, you will be able to increase your profit. Off-season fruits and vegetables are more expensive.

Give it a Try, and Good Luck!

Conclusions

Soil-based hydroponic cultivation allows cultivation in unfriendly environments or conditions unsuitable for the birth and growth of plants.

Another essential aspect, fundamental for fans of hydroponics, is the amount of water to be provided for irrigation: in traditional crops on the land, the amount of water necessary to be able to grow and fruit plants is much higher than that required from vegetables grown in hydroponics. In fact, it is calculated that the ratio is 10 (for traditional crops) to 1 (for hydroponic crops).

This is reflected both in the economic aspect and in the environmental issue. For this reason, hydroponic cultivation is also called hydroponic culture precisely because it affects different economic, social, and even cultural areas and has a decidedly limited ecological footprint.

The 21 little-known secrets of this guide will help you get the best out of your hydroponic garden.

Remember to continue studying, deepening, and testing using all the possibilities that this type of culture offers us.

Happy Growth!

Printed in Great Britain
by Amazon